INSIDE PASSAGE

INSIDE PASSAGE

LIVING WITH
KILLER WHALES,
BALD EAGLES, AND
KWAKIUTL INDIANS

MICHAEL MODZELEWSKI

HarperPerennial

A Division of HarperCollins*Publishers*

Portions of *Inside Passage* have appeared in slightly different form in *Outside* magazine, *Oceans* magazine, *Bird Watcher's Digest*, *Stories About Birds and Bird Watchers Anthology*, *Wine Country* magazine, and the *Napa Valley Times*.

A hardcover edition of this book was published in 1991 by HarperCollins Publishers.

HarperCollins books may be purchased for educational, business, or sales promotional use. For information, please write: Special Markets Department, HarperCollins Publishers, Inc., 10 East 53rd Street, New York, NY 10022.

First HarperPerennial edition published 1992.

Designed by Cassandra J. Pappas

The Library of Congress has catalogued the hardcover edition as follows:

Modzelewski, Michael, 1953–
    Inside passage : living with killer whales, bald eagles, and
Kwakiutl Indians / by Michael Modzelewski.—1st ed.
      p.   cm.
   ISBN 0-06-016533-2
   1. Inside Passage—Description and travel.   2. Inside Passage—
Social life and customs.   3. Natural history—Inside Passage.
4. Kwakiutl Indians.   5. Modzelewski, Michael, 1953– —Homes and
haunts—Inside Passage.   I. Title.
F1089.I5M63   1991
917.9804′5—dc20   90-55545

ISBN 0-06-092273-7 (pbk.)

92 93 94 95 96 AC/RRD 10 9 8 7 6 5 4 3

For all of the people,
worldwide, who are working
for the preservation of wildlife

CONTENTS

*"I want to speak with many things
and I will not leave this planet
without knowing what I came to find,
without solving this affair,
and people are not enough.
I have to go much farther
and I have to go much closer."*

—PABLO NERUDA

PRELUDE

For as long as I can remember, I've wanted to live on an island. On land surrounded by vast ocean, cast away from the crowds, dependent only on myself—that's a challenge I've always wanted to meet.

Paradise islands are as different as the dreamers who dream them. Feeling stifled in the city, my projections were not of white sand, swaying palm trees, lassitude under the sun. Rather, I pictured a northern island with an evergreen forest full of wild animals; cold, clear sea streaked with salmon; dark, brooding skies.

My dream grew, as I did, amid the steel towers of Cleveland, Ohio—where my father played professional football and then, after retiring, went into the restaurant business. I lived for the summers when we left the city to stay on our hundred-acre family farm—forty acres of which were unadulterated woods to explore. I went away to the University of Maryland on a football scholarship, but quit after my freshman year. I couldn't live up to the larger-than-life, nine-foot, blow-up photo of my All-American father above my locker. And instead of the fun and "it's *how* you play the game" of the high school gridiron, college football was big business, win at any cost, and when I found myself writing poetry instead of studying the massive playbook, I knew a large part of me was going unfulfilled and that it was time for a change.

I then traveled across Europe for two months with a backpack and a Eurailpass, visiting thirteen countries, learning that on a continent with a historical perspective, businessmen and professional athletes didn't necessarily hold the most revered positions. I roamed along streets and parks named after writers and artists. One evening, in a Paris sidewalk cafe, while trying to wrestle my thoughts into a blank journal, a French couple, in English, invited me over to join them for a drink. "As soon as I finish this," I said, lifting pen and paper above the stack of demitasse between us. "Ah—you're a *writer*!" they said in unison as if it were life's highest calling.

I returned to the United States, enrolling at Indiana University, majoring in English literature with a minor in art history. In the fourth week I was dismissed from my only creative writing class, a prophetic professor stating that I was "one of the savages" and "like Gauguin, you should live on an island . . . do nothing but write." After somehow graduating (never letting school get in the way of my education), I moved to Aspen, Colorado, determined to be both a ski bum and a writer. But what on earth should I write about?

Then one night at the Isis Theatre I saw the movie *Jeremiah Johnson*. Up on the screen, for two hours, I found what I had spent a year in Aspen looking for: raw, unharnessed wilderness and a chance for a young man to test himself down to the marrow. I came out of the theater a walking, talking double of Robert Redford's mountain man. I charged through my studio apartment, grabbing a sleeping bag on the way out—over the back deck to sleep in the snow alongside the Roaring Fork River, the temperature at five below that night. I froze but refused to give in, to sleep within four walls, a travesty after seeing that movie. The next day, I dressed warmly, put on my backpack, and traipsed up into the Rocky Mountains above town, trying to relive the cinematic scenes. But everywhere I turned, the mountains had been carved and groomed into ski runs with looming cables, fancy gondolas, and schussing crowds. Passing back through town, I saw Aspen as a false Shangri-la of discos, trendy restaurants, chic boutiques full of New Yorkers and Texans fresh off Learjets for a week of skiing, shopping, and high times. Yep—time to move on. But to where?

I sensed that the *where* would really determine *what* I wrote about, and I've always believed that every legitimate desire creates a magnetic vortex attracting the fulfillment of that need—if you put constant energy and faith into it. At night, while drifting off to sleep, my mind kept turning north, but then to choose and reach my destination I needed a guide, an emissary. I bumped into her, literally, some months later during the International Design Conference, a week-long annual event attracting architects, fashion designers, futurists, and innovators from all over the world for an exchange of ideas in Aspen. During a lunch break one day, it was announced that there would be a hang-gliding exhibition, with fliers coming down from the top of Ajax Mountain to land in the meadow. As I stepped backward with eyes to the sky, following the human kites, I bumped smack into another back. We both turned around at the same time and—*pow*—much love at first sight. Genevieve, a Frenchwoman, an architect from Vancouver. . . . Suddenly the Design Conference wasn't at all important. We skipped out during Rudi Gernreich's show of space-age swimsuits, heading up into the summer mountains to live like primitives, *fauves* wild with love. But she couldn't stay, had to get back to commissions in Vancouver. Then her daily letters insisted I come and visit. Pack on the back, thumb out, I hopped down the highway, pausing in Provo, Utah, for a visit to Sundance to try to see Robert Redford.

In Aspen I had worked as a copywriter for an environmental school and had sent Redford a big, visual layout board showing and describing Wildwood's potential magic—and requesting a sizable contribution to see it through. He replied that he was interested, and the director of the school and I arranged to meet with him at a reception after the Denver premier of *All the President's Men*. But with the crush of stargazers around him, there was no time to talk business, and he was off to Europe that night. But he had said, "Check with me in a month." So I did just that— but then didn't have time to prepare for what I was going to say, for as soon as I stepped away from my ride, there was Redford with his family coming out of the woods at the end of a hike. Before he disappeared, I brashly called, "Bob!"—stopping him in his tracks. After discussing the school, I told him how much *Jeremiah Johnson* meant to me. He took out a scrap of paper and a pen, drawing a map of where "some of the scenes were filmed here on the land," and he put an *X* over the best spot to camp. As I wandered through the actual sets, it was enough to almost forget about Genevieve! But on to Vancouver and a glorious week together sailing a ketch around the lower Inside Passage islands.

Spending time together—whether heeled-over at ten knots, anchored alone in remote bays, or wandering through the islands' small towns—it became clear that ours would not be a full-time relationship. Genevieve was committed to making her mark as an architect in Vancouver; I didn't want to live in a big city, but instead planned to continue my quest to find and experience total wilderness. We decided to concentrate solely on enjoying our moments together. I soon learned that some people appear in our lives briefly to connect us to other people or events that carry a lasting impact.

The night before I was to return to Aspen, the telephone rang in Genevieve's house. "Yes . . . oh, yes—Will— I remember! We met at Peggy's party. Well, I'd love to join you for dinner, but I have— Why don't *we* meet you? Okay? Fine, we'll be right over!" When she hung up, she smiled, nodding her head. "You are in for a treat, Michelito! An amazing man—he lives on his own island and sings to the killer whales and allows bees to make a hive in his coat pocket. . . . You will like each other, I know." As we drove over to the bus depot, I asked Genevieve to tell me more about this Will Malloff, but she wouldn't say anything, just kept smiling.

Malloff and I didn't begin under ideal circumstances. Island-bound for months without a woman, Malloff had taken a quick trip to town, looking for action—but then I was there in the way. But as we settled in over a Chinese dinner, Genevieve sat back, head swiveling as she watched Malloff and me link up with stories about panning for gold in the Yukon, mountain climbing, blacksmithing, Aspen, Swanson Island. Malloff told me about living on his own island in the Inside Passage. He painted paradise word pictures—very similar to the scenes that had flashed across the screen behind my eyes.

"Come up and see it," Malloff said as he stood up from the table. "It's two hundred miles north and about a hundred years back."

Prelude

I cracked open my fortune cookie: YOU ARE GOING ON A
JOURNEY TO AN EXOTIC LAND. A day later I hopped on a
northbound ferry and found Swanson Island.

Two kayaks were tethered on the beach. The door of
the small house was open. A young couple introduced
themselves and invited me in.

"Will's out fishing," Doug said.

Cheryl explained that they were paddling up the Inside Passage—the waterway from Seattle to Alaska. Doug
set out a platter of steamed clams. As we ate, I listened to
their tales of adventure.

"Ever been in a kayak?" Doug enquired.

"No."

"Let's go," he said through a smile.

We glided out with the tide. An immense school of
herring pulsed beneath us. A big salmon broke water. We
paddled around a rocky islet, surprising a seal: it flopped
high, then rolled smoothly into the sea.

Off in the distance, a whale spouted a plume of breath.
A bear lumbered out of deep forest onto a pebble beach,
rising up on its hind legs to sniff the air. A bald eagle soared
over our heads, then perched in a pine, watching us watch
the bear.

Above the sea were snow-capped mountains. A setting
sun and full moon shared the sky. I sipped fresh, cold air
that expanded my chest. The only sound was the sigh of the
sea over beach stones.

We turned back, aiming for the tiny buildings set in
amid towering cedar and fir trees. I looked around full
circle. Malloff's niche was the only sign of man.

"This stretch of water have a name?" I asked Doug.

"Blackfish Sound. *Blackfish* is the Kwakiutl Indian
name for the killer whale. This is one of their main breeding
grounds."

Malloff returned in a dory half filled with fish. "Soooo . . ."

I shook my head and waved my arms around. For the first time in my life, I was speechless, overcome by the wild perfection.

The kayakers moved on. I lingered. Alongside Malloff, for three weeks, I split wood, cleared trails, fished, and foraged. In the evenings we had survival "seminars," for I was intimidated by the sea. I had every right to be. The Inside Passage is thought by outsiders to be gentle ocean, calm corridors of water between island buffers. The reality is that the Passage contains some of the most dangerous water in the world. Those corridors can act as wind funnels, and the many islands jumble tides and stack up steep waves. In the snug cabin at night, I asked Malloff hundreds of questions about the sea's many moods that he had learned about over nine years on his island outpost.

Under his tutelage, I studied the tides, currents, waves, the dory's capabilities. Malloff built his work boat by hand—after apprenticing with the dory masters in Lunenburg, Nova Scotia. The dory's every reaction was engrained in Malloff's mind and he did his best to transfer that knowledge to me. Malloff showed me all the knots necessary to an islander and I practiced tying clove hitches and bowlines until I could do them automatically, without thought.

"It's paradise here—but in the next minute it'll try to kill you. The only way to survive is to always be prepared!" was Malloff's "mantra," which I took to heart.

During the day, Malloff pointed out the clouds to read: wind doggies, mare's tails, popcorn cumuli that preview the weather. I began memorizing the local nautical charts and the outboard motor manual. Amid our daily physical labors I kept asking him "What would you do out there if . . . ?" questions. Alone in the dory, I soon rode the massive waves as if they were tame horses.

One evening, Malloff asked me if I would watch over the place while he went away. "There's woods and ocean full of all you need."

At the end of the third week, as I watched the expanding wake of Malloff's departing speedboat, a keen sense of anticipation rose up within me. I had found a truly wild place and I was now alone to prove myself.

The richness of the actual wilderness far surpassed my wildest dreams.

1

WINTER SOLITUDE

I surfaced from sleep breathing with the surf.

My eyes opened to pale dawn. I lay still, strengthening with the increasing light.

I pushed off the quilt, went down the loft ladder, and hopped across a frozen floor to the airtight stove. I raked the embers together and added thick chunks of wood. I dressed in wool clothes and went outside, grabbing up the bucket and a hatchet.

As I straddled the creek, chopping through the ice, my father's words echoed in my ears: "Woodstove, kerosene lamps, outhouse, carry-in water . . . I worked hard all my life to get you past all that. But to me that was the Depression and it was forced on us. You're doing it by choice. Why?"

I had replied, "Sometimes you have to lower your standard of living to reach a higher level. . . ."

I carried the frigid water into the warming house. The

two dogs and the cat scampered in and nestled around the stove. Stepping over them, I removed the airtight lid and fit Will Malloff's giant frying pan into the round opening. Fresh eggs and wild boar bacon sizzled in the pan.

As I ate, I looked out the large windows, scanning the vast Sound. My eyes were drawn to movement—be it a flickering kingfisher or a breaching whale. As I sat back sipping hot tea, I gazed out upon the tremendous blend of ocean, islands, mountains.

The house sat up on a slope fifty feet above the sea. It was a small home—twelve feet across and thirty-four feet long. The surrounding immensity made a limited space not only tolerable but psychologically desirable. Like the animals with dens in the big woods, I welcomed this confinement, found it necessary to be able to leave the outer world completely, to nestle within a small, familiar space.

The wooden house imparted the secure feeling of being aboard a tightly built boat. The upper deck was the platform loft. In the midsection was the kitchen, the warm heart of a cold-coast home. The chugging woodstove was central and loomed large. Plates, cutlery, spices, glass jars of bulk food—all were shelved and racked shipshape. Up in the "bow" was a round table, six feet across and six inches thick, that Malloff had milled from a Mendocino redwood stump, then sanded and varnished until it glowed. The massive table was attached to a steel tire-changing stand, which in turn was bolted to the floor. The redwood round served as the basis for all meals, as chart table, writing desk, and dance floor—when we and guests got in the swing.

Between the big table and the front wall of tall windows was a daybed. The frame was rough-hewn alder slabs; the slim mattress was covered with a red Navajo blanket. It was a soft bench near the table for extra guests, or if you turned it the other way it became a plush observation deck. While supper was cooking, you could stretch out over Blackfish Sound to see bald eagles or killer whales on the prowl.

Twin panels of eight-foot-tall rectangular glass were set in the front wall, and another pair extended that openness out horizontally, one in each side wall. By moving your chair around the redwood circle, you could encompass most of the outer world.

Looking straight out the front window, you saw two small oval islands, solid with evergreens. They lay about one hundred yards offshore. No Name Island was at a forty-five-degree angle to the left, with Flower Island out at the same angle to the right. They sheltered the calm Freshwater Bay, to which the entries were three—through the wide center channel between No Name and Flower, or in the side narrows between each island and Swanson Island, upon which the house stood.

Beyond the two buffer islands stretched the open expanse of Blackfish Sound. Four miles distant sprawled the elongated Hanson Island, creating the low horizon. Behind it, out of sight, flowed Johnstone Strait. On the far side of that narrow sea was a wall of eight-thousand-foot mountains making up the northeast edge of Vancouver Island.

Looking out the front window, off in the far left corner, the end of Hanson and the tip of a sword-shaped island cut the narrow Blacknee Pass where the tides slammed the bulk of Blackfish Sound against Johnstone Strait. It was through this heaving gap that tugboats, freighters, and hotel-cruise ships passed on their way up to Alaska. Looking out from the table, the ships at first would appear as toy boats bobbing in the chop, then slowly increase to immense size, the big screws of the freighters vibrating the house windows as they plowed up the Sound.

Out of sight—flung away to the far right—a dribble of islands led to the open Queen Charlotte Sound, south of the Alaska marine border by about 250 miles.

Extending behind, or east, of Swanson Island is a vast archipelago containing a labyrinth of sounds, straits, canals, narrows, and channels, eventually leading to fjords that wind serpentinely into the coastal mountains. The British Columbia coastline curls in upon itself for 18,705 kilometers, a length equal to halfway around the earth at the equator.

Swanson Island (three and a half miles long and one and a half miles wide) is in the lower third of the Inside Passage, which extends nine hundred miles from the southern tip of Vancouver Island up to Glacier Bay, Alaska.

Ten thousand years ago, the passage was buried under an ice sheet nearly one mile thick. The enormous glaciers left landscapes mighty and bold.

The Inside Passage breeds size into many of its elements. Forests of cedar trees tower up to 250 feet. Brown bears stand 10 feet tall and weigh nearly a ton. One king salmon can cover your kitchen table.

The giant scale, and vast contrast between mountains and sea, to my eyes made the Inside Passage dwarf the rest of the world. It brought to mind the music of Wagner, with the Passage containing the same colossal themes. *The Ring* could have been forged in the bowels beneath Blackfish Sound. Valhalla could be found topping any one of the fjordic mountains. "The Ride of the Valkyries" could be orchestrated by the sweep of the northern lights.

The many islands are actually mountaintops, the slopes submerged during melts of earlier ice ages. Inland, the ice continues its carving. The fjord waters are opulent green with glacier "milk"—ground-up continent in suspension.

The sky brooded in chiaroscuro. Sunlight pierced

clouds in shafts so tall and brilliant that it was as if I saw Jacob's ladder. Twelve feet of rain poured over the land in a year, nearly all of it falling in the winter. Fierce winds constantly erupted the sea. Then there were obliterating fog, whirlpools, water spouts, and snow that simultaneously melted into the ocean while burying islands deep white. It was grand drama that never ceased to amaze, frighten, delight me.

I sat there in the tiny house perched on an island-top mountain, looking out over this Inside Passage, seeing no people, no other houses for mile after mile of wilderness. "The Only Man Left on Earth" was a scenario I had imagined to survive the crowded city. That dream, suddenly, I was living.

Fresh snow mornings, I walked deep into the forest. The tall cedars were clotted heavy with snow. Snow showed the spidery lines of tree bark and fluffed full each crevice in every rock.

I opened my mouth and inhaled drafts of air, chewing fresh cold tinged with tree resin. A newly minted world.

The buried forest muffled all sound. Silence reigned. It was a total, pure absence I had never heard before. In the city, quiet is constantly assaulted by machines. In this white womb, the only repetitive sound was my heartbeat, emphasizing the silence.

On my silent tramps, I pursued Socrates' advice to "know thyself." Like a prospector, I picked and shoveled beneath my surface and uncovered my worth. For uninterrupted hours I listened to subterranean voices that had previously been drowned in urban din.

Thought mosaics completed themselves deep within. A missing iota materialized in the quiescence: exactly why past relationships hadn't worked; what I should have said to improve a particular situation—lessons that were held back until they had unconfined time and space to expand into knowledge. During the winter, the snow walker was often shaken by a jolt of understanding. "*A-ha! Ha, yes!*" I spouted, as the missing "peace" fell into place. My ebullience rushed through the slumbering woods to ring off granite bluffs in great peals. Zen laughter—once so forcefully decisive that it shook snow off a low-slung branch.

In the island clearings snow stretched like sheets of white papyrus. The smooth surfaces were occasionally broken by hieroglyphic markings. I read natural history by studying the imprints. The snow showed the press of outstretched wings, parallel dots, then a deeper fan of feathers . . . and dribbles of blood. On its second stab, an owl had captured a rodent. In the center of a small clearing, the snow wore a dimple that flashed iridescent colors. I trudged to the source to find, down in the white, a blazing abalone shell. An eagle or raven had eaten a meal and then discarded the plate.

One morning I followed deer prints off into the woods. The deer had walked a deliberate course: no side trips, no feeding digressions. The tracks ended in the lee of a toppled cedar. A bare patch of loam showed where the deer had slept.

Fresh exit tracks meandered across the snow and then stopped abruptly. The tracks began again six feet away in the opposite direction. Something had so spooked the deer that it jumped completely around in midstride. Sprint prints moved out twelve feet apart with the deer bounding clear over big logs and bushes. It touched down just once on the wide hiking path.

As I followed, I noticed that the snow had been disturbed differently higher up the hill. With all my senses probing, I moved upward to see wide tracks cutting through the snow: cougar prints—so fresh they appeared to quiver.

I bolted back down the hill—both pleased and some-what frightened that a cougar roamed the upper island.

The clear winter days were polished off by dazzling sunsets. I sat at the round table with two fingers of rum and watched the sun stain sky and sea with flaming colors. I thought of how no artist has come close to re-creating this beauty in a painting.

As the intense hues waned, the sun gathered force for a grand finale. The disk sank behind Elephant Mountain, casting it in bronze, the mountain glowing as if fired from within.

I poured another slosh of rum and scanned the evening sky for a show of a different sort. Occasionally my vigil would be rewarded with the northern lights: a cold fire of red and iridescent green shimmering through the dark sky. It was then that my solitude would turn against me. I would ache for company, someone to share the magic beauty.

The aurora borealis now stormed south, leaving the sky an empty bowl. The sea was motionless. The air, a still mass. Cold froze all movement. Cold pushed through the windows and occupied the house.

Two chilled dog noses nudged my hands.

I stoked the woodstove, lit the kerosene lamps, and proceeded to cook dinner. After eating, I took out pen and paper, writing long letters to distant friends (I would save the letters for passing boats to mail), trying to bring them into my new world.

When I ran out of words, I put on a warm coat and went outside. There was silence that roared. There was a night sky so luminous that my eyes opened wide and star-light splashed in like a fine rain.

I thought myself into the Milky Way, linking the

whorls of light into constellations of my own design. I orbited with planets gleaming like multicolored sapphires. I rode shooting stars that etched fiery trails across the black dome.

I didn't end at my skin. I expanded into outer space, which formed my inner being.

With that realization, I came back to earth. I looked over my shoulder through the darkness at the buttery glow of the lamps behind frosted glass. I felt intensely alone, intensely alive. Under all of the universe, sprawled and spangled above, the cabin shone like a small answer.

November was consumed by monsoons. Day after day the rain was driven sideways by raging winds. Low, sodden clouds dumped rain as they sailed over the chaotic waves. The forest firs were bent like long bows, their branches arrows against the wind. From the waves and trees came a roar that pulverized the ears.

Feeling as outrageous as the weather, one day I dashed naked out onto a rocky point and clung to a gnarled fir. The wind pummeled my body, trying to wrench me from the stronghold. I opened my mouth and King Lear spouted: "*Blow Ye Winds! Rage, Blooooo . . .*" The mad wind sliced off wave crests, pelting me with brine.

As I clung to the buckled tree, I squinted up at a bald eagle. Into the wind—wings outstretched—it held itself still in the rolling sky. Bored with such an easy conquest, it turned on a gust and sailed past me.

At first I welcomed being stormbound. Because the house was on a rise so near the water, the land-boat gave me the feeling of being at sea but without actual concern about the waves. I sat warm and snug at the table, woodstove chugging at my back, coffee and rum close at hand. Through the tall windows I watched in comfort as the procession of storms blasted across Blackfish Sound.

What phantasmagoric forms the wind-whipped sea assumed! Herds of white-maned creatures climbed each others' backs in wild, uncontrollable fury.

The sky seemed to collapse from within, as if the very matter that composed it was fed into the locomotive wind. The air darkened to the purple-black of a bruise as the wind roared by, smashing through island forests. Loud cannonades punched the ears as trees were toppled.

I thought I sat aloof, high and dry amid the maelstrom, but one day I found myself clutching the table in a white-knuckled grip. As the wind drove the high tide far up the beach, waves broke under the house, spattering spume hard against the windows. The wind then slipped down the stove pipe and inverted the fire. A long tongue of flame shot out the air vent, nearly setting my seat afire!

I poured water into the stove and paced back and forth to stay warm. This *cheechako* (Chinook jargon for "newcomer") swore it was the end of the world. There was a malevolence in the air; I tasted it—like cold copper on the tongue. It was as if Nature was punishing the world, as if pent-up anger finally found release, as if the throttle of rage was wide open and stuck there. Day after day the wind attacked. It tore anything weak from its moorings: trees, birds, kelp, seals were yanked like weeds. I watched the big firs and cedars, the whales and eagles flailing away. For even the strongest, the unrelenting wind tested all the way down to the bottom of their strength. But even the wind needed a rest. After ten straight days, the racing velocity finally slowed.

The black sky softened to a wash of gray. Shredded clouds collected themselves. Through ragged holes, sunbeams swept spotlights across a pewter sea. Waves slid back and forth, restless with residue energy. There was no relaxation. Nervous tension knotted the air. This was but a brief reprieve. The forests, sea, animals, and I waited—

braced for the next blast. Sure enough, the wind returned full force—at fifty to sixty knots it blew up Blackfish Sound.

During the tempestuous nights I turned to books. I had brought a suitcase full of thick tomes that I never had time for. How marvelous now to read Joseph Conrad with Blackfish Sound yawing with the words! However, after a steady diet of Conrad, Melville, and Jack London, I felt constricted. Their tales inspire one to perform feats of bravado. But with the outer world blown to smithereens, my proving ground was limited to the tiny house.

There was no letup in the storms. Day and night, night and day, the winds and rains raged. After the constant confinement, I felt victimized, rendered powerless by the power of the weather. Never before had I encountered such raw, walloping forces.

During a brief limbo, with the latest storm spent, I thought that no wind could ever again blow that hard. Never could so much rain fall so continuously. *Yes, this is the end of it. Now I'll see the sun.* But then another gale arrived with such might that it made the previous blow seem a feeble breeze, mere drizzle.

I grew agitated and restless. I had absorbed all that kinetic energy and couldn't release it. I no longer watched the storms as a detached bystander. The tempests raged inside of me.

When Coyote, the trickster of Indian lore, was asked the meaning of loneliness, he put a single pebble into an empty gourd and shook the gourd for many days. I felt like that pebble, bouncing off the walls of the house.

Time turned into Dali's soft clocks. It was night all day and the darkness dragged on endlessly. Sleeping in fits and starts, I listened to the wind surround the house, grab the edges, shake it from all sides. The rain hit like lead beads. I was convinced that never again would I see the sun. Memorable sunrises and sunsets repeated themselves fast forward on the screen behind my eyes; I spun in the swirl of fanning colors.

I finally discovered a remedy, a release. Exercise broke the cabin fever. I disciplined myself to do two hundred pushups, two hundred situps, and a long run every day come high tide or hell water! I ran over the beaches, leaning through the wind wall, punching a path in the horizontal rain, fighting for oxygen in air that seemed all water. I hurdled through fields of driftwood flung up by the crazed sea. I chugged through bogs of loose stones, and sprinted over hard-packed sand.

Running with the wind at my back, I surged forward like a surfer riding the crest. I leapt over the raging creek—a broader jump every day as the swelling torrent gouged away the bank. I finished the run with an all-out kick, and then did twenty chin-ups on a heaving tree branch.

Back inside, I poured hot water into a tin tub and bathed. My body alive and brain renewed, the house walls seemed to move apart. Wind and rain became merely background music.

One clear afternoon, I didn't run alone. As I came out of a tunnel of trees onto a beach, I heard the whir of wings. I looked up. A bald eagle was flying, about thirty feet above me. I veered away from what I thought was an attack. The eagle followed, all seven feet of wings unfurled. I swerved back down the beach but the eagle copied my dodge. I sprinted. The eagle flapped, staying directly over me.

I dashed my fingers through my hair, thinking that I carried a bit of fish, a piece of salmon that I had eaten earlier—but my hair was clean. I snapped my head back and stared at the raptor, trying to discern what it wanted with me.

Big eagle eyes offered no answers. But as I kept staring into the sun circles, a thought repeated: *See yourself.*

What I saw shook me. There on the sand was my

shadow, and attached to the torso were wings. As I ran on, the eagle stayed directly above me, its wings fixed to my shadow. As I marveled at the extension, my legs seemed to fall away. I felt light and detached, as if gravity had loosened its hold, as if the wings were my own.

I was overwhelmed by the same sensation of self-powered flight that I had experienced in my dreams. But this was daylight and my eyes were wide open! It was dream come true, myth made real.

No freak coincidence. If the eagle had crossed my shadow for a second or two, coincidence I would have called it. But the eagle deliberately kept its wings fixed to my torso as I ran. When I saw and felt the eagle's aim, the connection jolted me into a "separate reality," as Castaneda called it. The man was inside the eagle watching the runner fly.

I soared through another tunnel of trees. When I came out the other side, I felt that I was landing, coming down. I looked up—the eagle was gone.

I stopped running and walked slowly back over the path, thinking about the flight, the union with the eagle. Then the jittery voice from the top of my brain cut in: *Hold on, you're getting carried away. Things like that just don't happen in this day and age!* Then a calm voice from within my body said: *You are not in that day and age. You are here. You are getting carried away. Accept it. Live a life worthy of it.*

My thoughts turned to the Indians who had gone on vision quests. In isolation, an individual purified himself so that he might gain insight into his future. Usually in a dream, but sometimes while the youth was awake, an animal appeared to him acting in a symbolic manner. If the seeker trusted what he saw, the visionary animal then guided his life.

I felt certain that I had been given my totem. The eagle had appeared as an Animal of Power. It pointed my Way.

*   *   *

The eagle was a good omen. Along with regarding it as my totem, I took it as a sign that I belonged, was accepted by this strangely powerful world. The next lesson I learned was that the North has a capricious nature. Just when I had steeled myself to the winter, the storms and cold suddenly ceased. A chinook (Chehalis for "snow eater") wind coursed across the island.

The house felt like an overheated oven. I shut down the woodstove and threw open the windows. Then I monitored the outside temperature. In two hours, the thermometer's red line lifted from forty to nearly seventy degrees. The warm wind delivered spring into the dead of winter.

I felt light-headed, full of mirth. I pulled off all my clothes and started up the high trail wearing only rubber gum boots.

The smooth path was too tame. I plunged off into a sea of salal bushes, welcoming the slash of thorny leaves on wool-smothered skin. I rubbed my back against the rough trunk of a cedar and scrubbed arms and legs with big handfuls of moss. I galloped through a shallow swamp, kicking up mud all over my body. The warm wind immediately dried the patches into wild tattoos.

I was free. No storms, house, clothes, books. Totally unbound. No mind—all sensation.

The sun's rays touched down with substantial heat. I pressed my chest against a bulge of granite and felt warmth fill me as helium does a balloon. I walked out to the edge of the bluff and looked over a blue sea studded with green islands, and mountains looming high and white above the distant mainland. After a long look, I closed my eyes and slowly inhaled, feeling the images, the colors spreading within . . . holding the breath, the wild beauty . . . then letting it stream, leaving each cell, every atom, charged with a sparkling equilibrium.

A few days after my wild roaming, a Kwakiutl Indian, Larry Joseph, came ashore. Over coffee, he asked where Wolf was—Wolf being his name for Will. I found it difficult to both listen and look at him. I couldn't monitor the audio because of the visual—a person actually *being* there, when for so long those chairs were empty. As Emerson said, "I can't hear what you are saying because who you are thunders so loudly."

The Kwakiutl wanted to know how I had come to live on the island. There was an abrupt, gruff edge to all his questions. When his investigation was over, as he stood up to leave, he stared at my many books stacked on the daybed.

"You guys college—all same. Load down wit knowleeg but no wisdom. You no survive here. You end up burn'n dos books to try to keep alive. I be by neks time to pick up you bones," he said while looking around the place as if it were already his.

As his skiff droned away, his parting words echoed inside my head, chilling me all the way through. I sat back down, wondering what I had gotten myself into. *Maybe he's right—maybe I'm in way over my head.* . . . But then, deep down, I felt a surge of confidence. I knew that Malloff wouldn't have left me alone if I couldn't hold down the fort.

As Malloff had told me, the fact that a white man had paid hard-earned money for a deed to island land meant little to many Kwakiutls. Their view was that you were trespassing, or if they liked you, you were "visiting" on land that rightfully belonged to them. The aggressive A.I.M.—American Indian Movement—had Kwakiutl members. A white landowner who bad-mouthed the Indians would be driven out by young raiding parties flexing their Red Power.

During the winter days, I set out to prove to the Indians that even a college kid overburdened with knowledge could live up to their demanding world. Larry Joseph issued a challenge and I would answer it to the best of my abilities, and what I didn't know I would learn along the way.

A few weeks after his first visit, Joseph came by in a herring skiff. I was out on the log raft, cleaning a lingcod I had just caught. In the bow of Joseph's boat, amid a jumble of equipment, was an imposing black bucket. He saw me eyeing the empty container.

"Come by to colleck you bones," the Indian said as he looked over the big fish, then tilted his head to see me in a new way. "But you look you survive good."

I turned the fish and slashed off a long, thick fillet and held it out to him. He took the meat without a word but the repercussions of what he had seen and received spread rapidly.

Basil Ambers, the "chief" of the wild-island Indians, came by. They had let the wind and rain and isolation work on me, and if I proved tough enough—then I belonged. By the warm look in Basil's eyes, I knew I had emerged from the rite of passage. I invited him in and we talked for hours like old friends. During Basil's many visits, he taught me an encyclopedia set of Kwakiutl knowledge and lore. I learned why when traveling the Inside Passage you should look over your shoulder at the outlines of the islands—so when you run into fog you can find your way home by the slightest silhouettes. He showed me the five hand waves to silently signal the different types of salmon to a fishing partner: the moves—perfect swimmings of each fish. He told me that "old man's beard"—the coarse clumps of moss hanging in trees—will start a fire out in the rain, the only material in the woods that flames instantly, even if wet. I learned the meanings behind Kwakiutl myths, what song to sing when going after halibut, Potlatch dance steps.

Thanks to Basil Ambers and other Kwakiutls, this tenderfoot now had a firmer stance in the wild world.

*   *   *

The only danger I felt was the threat of a careless accident. An islander constantly uses tools—ax, chainsaw, fire, fishhooks—that can reverse into self-inflicting weapons. Before every activity, I consciously scouted for potential dangers.

Once you inform your body that there is no hospital nearby, you suddenly possess amazing coordination. Each move is deliberately sure. There is no slack in you, for all systems are alert. It's exhilarating to live tuned to such a keen awareness.

In dangerous undertakings, like falling a crooked tree, I discovered that I could split my personality. One part of me chopped the tree, while another "me" stood by, on guard.

The nearest neighbor was Alec Stuart, a retired logger, caretaking Berry Island four miles away. In case of a medical emergency, four miles is a few minutes away in the city. But without a telephone and pavement to race across, those four sea miles, on a stormy day or against a heavy ebb tide, could be a near insurmountable distance.

Living with the threat of danger is what made life so exciting, such a high-voltage experience. On a wilderness island, to a great extent, you relinquish control. Nature rules. It forms the questions that you must answer to survive.

I was totally tested one day. I had gotten up early to attempt a ten-mile crossing of Blackfish Sound and Johnstone Strait to meet a man who had offered to teach me to scuba dive. At first light, I poked my head outside for the "weather report." Without television's high-tech, multicolored satellite maps, I had to rely on more primitive indicators. The tall pine trees were still, not a needle moving, and the sea was solid on the beach. It looked to be a safe morning to travel.

I dressed warmly and started out in Malloff's seventeen-foot dory, powered by a small outboard engine. As I crossed the placid Sound, I sensed something was wrong. It was the calm—there was too much of it. The sea and air were lifeless. No fish. No birds. No sounds. A total suspension of movement. It was as if Nature were holding its breath. Uneasy, I continued on across the glass sea.

I was nosing out into Johnstone Strait when suddenly the wind erupted with a rage that can only originate from calm. I was caught flat-footed in a fifty-knot gale.

I tried to quarter into the waves but they threatened to topple into the open boat. I cast off hope of reaching my destination. To stay alive, I swung the dory around to run with the heaving sea.

A wave lifted the boat up, carried her forward at breakneck speed, then abruptly dropped her. The following wave hurled the dory even higher. I crouched low into the horse stance—a kung fu fighting position. My bowed legs acted as shock absorbers that balanced the erratic force of the elevator waves.

One hand gripped the tiller, the other wiped spindrift from my eyes. I looked across vast miles of rolling, roaring whitecaps. There were no other boats. The sun was shining. The wind swept the air crystal clear. Snow-dusted mountains glistened on the distant mainland.

Nearby were the mountains of Vancouver Island. My eyes picked along the rock walls for an opening, a notch, but there wasn't the slightest lee to duck into. I felt hollow with fear. I couldn't believe that I was actually out there. Man had no place in that tumultuous scene.

If you go in, you'll last maybe five minutes in forty-two-degree water. I looked at my wetsuit—a rubber shadow—in repose against the bow stem. But I couldn't leave the tiller. I looked over my shoulder and cringed. Consecutive walls of water loomed high above. To boost my courage, I shouted: "*Wild broncs—ride 'em out one at a time!*"

But conditions grew worse. The tide was changing. The jumble of islands turned outgoing ocean into rivers that crashed against the running sea, tossing up haystack waves that twisted the dory until she groaned. I expected the planks to split at any moment, but somehow the cedar flexed, deflecting defeat.

As I was battered in the gauntlet, I wished I could shut my eyes. The sight of those crazed waves was almost enough to rip the nerves out of my body. But there was no time to flinch. I was the ballast for the boat. How my legs helped balance the blows determined whether we stayed up—or went over.

My heart pumped into overdrive, charging my being with surges of electric energy. I tingled with both fear and exhilaration as we fought through yet another clash of waves.

The dory burst out of the haystacks to sudden calm on a flat, circular patch of sea. But the circle announced a power unto itself. The dory rocked side to side and then was spun around in tight turns like a toy boat with the drain open. The vortex yanked the boat down, burying the hull half under. I cut the racing engine to an idle. The dory lifted as if a suction seal had been broken. The whirlpool gave us a final spin and then spat us out.

I dropped to a knee, shaking, spent—but pulled myself up. The dory kept me going. I marveled at the low shelter around me. *How can it still be holding together? How, after attacks from such forces?*

No time for thinking. I sped all energy into the present moment.

The engine's throttle was at the end of the tiller arm—a twist-grip in my fist. As one wave dropped us, I gunned the outboard to get up on the back of the next monster.

Once the sea heaved and the wind hit, I twisted the engine down to a trickle. My fate was literally in my hand, for if I timed the speed too fast, I'd pitchpole the boat. If I cut it too slow, then the following sea would swamp us.

I didn't know that I knew what to do until I did it. Instinctive knowledge, buried deep down, rose to the occasion.

On top of the cresting waves, the wind had a clear shot at me. I tried to duck it by huddling down on the plank seat, but from low down I couldn't see ahead. I stood back up. I was wearing a coat with an outer layer of windbreaker nylon. But nothing could break this wind. The gusts flapped and thrummed that nylon, turning me into a human sail. It hit with strength to move my 180 pounds. I thought of removing the coat, but then I would freeze, so I wrestled against the blows.

I anchored my weight into my feet and curled my toes like grapples into the wood bottom—but the wind drove me forward. Just when my leg muscles were utterly taxed from the resistance, the dory skittered down a wave into a trough.

I sucked a deep breath and quickly gathered myself for the next round. I stole a second to take a wide view. The sky had darkened to deep purple. Tattered clouds blew by like tumbleweeds.

From a wave top, I looked down and saw a big log rolling in the trough. I tilted the outboard out of the water a split second before the dory's flat bottom hit and skidded over the log.

Bad had become worse and worse had become disaster. The outboard engine was knocked off! The continuous pounding had loosened the bracket screws and a cross-wave wrenched off the engine. The sudden falling weight nearly pulled me overboard. Buckled in half, down on my knees, I lifted with all my strength and the motor came up . . . sputtering.

The dory turned broadside in the trough. I slammed the engine over the transom, swung the tiller to port, gunned the throttle, and ducked.

The wave broke. As the sea roared in my ears, reality was shattered. No longer in control, my mind kaleido-scoped, rapidly tossing up the highs and lows of my life on the screen behind my eyes. After the last past insight, I then foresaw myself falling into the sea, crawling up, reaching for the boat or that log. But then the cold took hold and I saw my head nodding to the water. A last look up at Elephant Mountain, and then I pulled the wave over me like a shroud. . . .

But then I felt the wind on the back of my neck. I lifted my head. Miraculously, the dory was only half full and the outboard engine was still alive! Land was in sight. I grabbed the bailer and scooped out the sea as I steered, surfing the waves to Pepper Point on Cormorant Island. A small crowd of Indians and whites were waiting to catch the dory as she was flung ashore.

As I stepped out onto terra firma, they looked at me as if I were a ghost.

"You got be crazy be'in oud dere," mumbled an old Kwakiutl.

"I spotted you from the kitchen window. Said to Maureen, 'I don't believe it, but there's a small boat bucking those waves!' "

"Coast Guard radio reports winds at fifty gusting to eighty knots. . . ."

How wonderful to see human faces—but their voices sounded far away. I must have been in shock—locked into the life-and-death battle. I remember being led into a house . . . a warm kitchen. . . .

I woke up in bed. It was late and quiet in the night. There was no wind. How good it felt to be lying still, warm, and dry—done in, but alive! Quivering muscles shook the mattress, sending my mind back over the battle.

I remembered how my eyes were so keen that they seemed to slow each wave to film its dimensions. In split seconds my brain scanned the pictures, then fired off the proper touch to my hand on the tiller-throttle. Fueled by fear, my eyes went as far as zoom lenses, and to be absolutely sure, they overcompensated. I could actually see into the waves, spotting bubbles, shreds of bark, even pine needles in the watery haystacks.

I recalled all the tons of pounding force the ocean hit the dory with. I thought of Will Malloff's hands that built a boat stronger than that strength.

I knew that from now on I would live in a different manner. Having faced death, I would never take life for granted. I would savor each and every moment, play the center of the note, as musicians say.

I attempted to raise my left hand off the mattress—but it wouldn't budge. Like talons, my fingers were frozen in the curled throttle position. That one hand had pulled a heavy engine up from the sea . . . but now the loan of power had to be repaid.

I reflected on the death premonition. I had always programmed myself to go out swinging—to knock out a few of the Grim Reaper's teeth, never ever surrender. But as the wave roared over me, it was as if I was prepared to die. That fact shook my mind as much as my body shook the bed.

With my subconscious seemingly shaken loose, aroused by the battle, I then realized that the remote island had shaped me into a far different person. Partaking directly of Nature's rhythms had taught me a great truth: death is transformation instead of termination; the end is a new beginning. . . .

2

SPIRIT WRESTLER

first met Will Malloff, of all places, in the Greyhound bus station in downtown Vancouver. He was in a flowing tide of people, and without a description to go by, immediately I picked him out of the crowd. I was drawn to a most unusual, powerful-looking man: a Cro-Magnon in street clothes; Russia on two legs.

Forty-four years old, Malloff was six feet two and weighed 245 pounds, with arms big as legs and legs like tree stumps. He had a wide Slavic face with high cheekbones and forehead, deep dark eyes, a thick jaw, and wavy black hair combed straight back. As he spoke I stared at his hands: they were huge and dented with fresh cuts, old scars, a fingernail blackened on each hand. He had a way of perking his right hand into the air as he was speaking, twisting the wrist, then flicking out a big finger to emphasize a point—so not only did you hear what he was saying but you could feel his thoughts thump into you. His words were a curious mix of old-time logger sayings, hippie lingo ("far out," "wow," "wasted"), and an extensive vocabulary from explorations into matters scientific and psychological. A trace of old Russian interrupted his Canadian accent when he became excited about a topic. It was clear that Malloff wasn't formally educated but had taught himself things those in schools would never know. I saw Malloff, who had a gargantuan appetite for life and self-taught expertise in many areas, as a sort of human brontosaurus—a species of man supposed to be extinct long ago.

When Malloff was on the island, our days were spent doing hard, physical labor, but then we made the evenings totally different. We got out cigars and Celebes coffee, converting the small shack into a European café as we talked far into the night.

Malloff spoke of how he found the island. While living in a Mendocino redwood forest with his wife Georgeanna, during the late 1960s, they were looking to surpass the stagnating hippie movement and set up their own utopia elsewhere. One day they saw "Island For Sale" in the newspaper and went up the coast with a friend, Michael Macy (of Macy's department stores), to check it out. Malloff had never before been on an island and wasn't at all familiar with the sea, but one look around at the beauty and immense potential convinced the three of them that the wild island was their new home. But shortly after the deal was closed Macy wanted out, so the island belonged to the Malloffs alone. When the couple stepped out of Will's handmade dory onto the island with a tent and chainsaw, they plunged into work, clearing an opening in the rain forest, collecting outcast buildings from logging camps: a timekeeper's shack converted into the main house, a three-room bunkhouse for guests and machine shop, small buildings to convert into a dory shop, and an artist's studio for

Georgeanna, all of which they brought in by barge and pushed into place with a small Caterpillar tractor. The tractor Malloff bought for hand logging: selectively cutting, then hauling the timber into a side bay, where with cable he bundled the logs into sections for a tug to tow to a Vancouver sawmill. As Georgeanna converted home and shop interiors and cleared and planted a half-acre garden, Malloff raced to put wood in the water—barely keeping up with the island's steep payments, and learning that the more you free yourself from conventional life, the harder you have to work to earn that freedom.

But after a couple of years of nonstop effort, they had established a stronghold. They showed visitors what two people could accomplish undistracted by trivialities. They produced a cornucopia of food: a fresh array of seafood and garden greens; wild mushrooms, onions, herbs. Georgeanna planted an orchard of fruit trees. There were geese and pheasants fattening in pens, chickens for eggs, Rhodesian Ridgeback dogs to keep away wild intruders. The machine, blacksmith, and dory shops were in full production, and Georgeanna had the perfect studio: inspiration out every window as she carved abstract totem poles, a stone rose, Pan in blond cedar, displaying her creations throughout the forest. A carved seal she had placed on the side of a rocky islet stopped even the killer whales, as they repeatedly leaped up for a closer look.

Then just when everything was going good, their marriage went bad. Georgeanna had left months before I arrived, settling in Vancouver and accepting wood-carving commissions.

When Malloff was on the island, I slept in a makeshift room off to one side of the bunkhouse. In the center, as you walked in, was a barrel woodstove, the pipe enclosed in a hot-water sleeve; a washing machine; and shower. Outside, a small gas engine sucked water out of a deep pool in the creek, pumping full a two-hundred-gallon tank on a hillside that gravity-fed water into the bunkhouse through narrow plastic pipes above ground. A small diesel generator provided the electrical power for all the machines. To the right as you walked in was Malloff's main shop, filled with every tool imaginable, from hair-thin screwdrivers to a massive drill press, from assorted grinders to a precision lathe. Shelves held dozens of pipe tobacco cans full of nuts and bolts, every size. Walls were covered with loose chain for saws, chalked designs for tool inventions. On the center bench was a beautiful alder slab table under construction or the prototype for a revolutionary chair. The remote island was really the laboratory of a mechanical wizard and woodworker extraordinaire. When Malloff looked at things he broke them down in his mind, always seeing form as process. He got me to look at objects the same way—from the inside out: seeing beauty, appreciating what before was just lifeless metal. Malloff collected tools the way I did books.

One day I asked him, "Say your shop caught fire and you could dash in for just one single tool—what would it be?"

He laughed a deep rumble, as if already prepared. He unsnapped the black leather holster attached to his belt and removed a large pair of Vise-Grips. "Drop me into any junkyard with these, and I'll build a palace!"

Some days we worked in the open-air blacksmith shop with a set of implements, once used to service clipper ships on the Saint Lawrence Seaway, which Malloff had bought at an antiques auction. I pushed the handle on the bellows, feeding air into the fire pit as he forged a fireplace poker or tempered a steel blade for a skinning knife. He showed me how fire spreads a prism of colors across steel. "And depending on what grade you're repairing, you quench when it glows a purple. . . ."

It was like seeing Vulcan at his forge with the fire roaring, cinders snapping as Malloff shoved long tongs into the burning heap: yanking out a giant door hinge, reaching without looking for a hammer, bringing both together atop the anvil in a ringing peal, splitting the glowing tip, then pushing it down over the horn, the molten iron ends curling open like smooth taffy. He paused, waiting for the red hue to fade pink, then plunged the ornamental hinge into a barrel of water. Over the hiss of steam, he said, "Only takes a second, but lasts forever," lifting the hinge, admiring his design.

Then early one morning, he knocked on the bunk-house door. "Michael—let's go hunting!"

"For what?"

"Dory wood. Come on—tide's just right."

We went out in dory number one—the original—riding up close to the beaches, Malloff stopping to pick through the driftwood, collecting a sorry-looking lot of bent limbs, forked trunks, or climbing up a hillside with the small chainsaw to cut out the curved stump of a Douglas fir. Back home, I spread the gnarled wood above the beach while Malloff assembled the "Alaska Mill": basically, a chainsaw fitted sideways into roller bars and slide adjustments so you can cut precision lumber directly from a downed tree. I watched in amazement as he swung the roaring mill through the "natural knees"—shaping curved ribs for the new dory. The grizzled wood held beautiful grain within. I ran my hand over the cuts—slick smooth. The Alaska mill never worked properly until Malloff designed and patented a ripping chain that could slice, from heartwood, interior house beams sawmill smooth. For his dories, based on the Lunenburg, Nova Scotia, design, Malloff used a variety of Northwest coast woods, placing the wood perfectly into the form: red cedar for the lapstrake planking and first bottom, strong Douglas fir for the second bottom and ribs, ironlike yew wood for the stern and bow stem, lightweight Sitka spruce for oars. All of the wood Malloff found and milled himself. The only materials he needed to buy were a couple pounds of nails.

Working hard day after day, we didn't want to break the productive mood for a trip to town for supplies. We had enough food, but for the evening café we had to split the last cigar in half and hit bottom in the coffee can. But we were plenty happy to drink the water that poured from a spring-fed creek into the house through a hose bent into the sink, returning it to the creek unless you caught the flow in a kettle or glass. It was pure "sweet water," as sailors call it. Malloff explained that most of the surrounding islands were uninhabited due to a total lack of freshwater springs. There were four gushers on Swanson and, as local legend had it, before Captain Vancouver sailed south to drop his name, he asked the Kwakiutls where he could tank up on drinking water. They directed him to where we sat, which the explorer then named Freshwater Bay.

Malloff walked back to the closet and returned with a battered twelve-string Martin guitar. He pulled his chair back from the table and sat down. He hunched over the guitar, his big body and face settling into granite as only his hands moved, strumming jazz and blues runs he had gathered from traveling the open road. His range was amazing. He played and sang everything from

> "Five foot two
> Eyes of blue
> Oh what five foot two could do!
> Has anybody seen my gal. . . ."

to somber songs in Russian that sounded like Dostoyevsky written for the guitar. Unable to follow the words, I received all the feeling: full of the suffering, pain, and enduring strength that is Russia.

Malloff set the guitar down and talked about the Dukhobors, whose name is Russian for "spirit wrestler." The sect was founded in 1750, professing to follow the inner light in interpreting the Scriptures. They denied the authority of temporal government, refused military service, and followed the leadership of inspired prophets. Czarist Russia was not the ideal place for Dukhobor pacifism and stubbornness. Suffering persecution, they were forced into Turkey. But then Tolstoy took up their cause, raising funds for them to settle on the open prairies of Canada. In 1890, Malloff's grandfather landed in Saskatchewan.

"In the early days," Malloff told me, "before the gardens and wheat crops started producing, the men had to work on the railroad or away in the mines, so the women hitched themselves to the plows—busting sod. . . . I was raised in Alberta in the Dukhobor traditions, lived right in the colony but then got out when the leaders got corrupt."

Malloff talked about protests—Dukhobor style. "The militant sect fights injustice by taking off their clothes—a big gang goes naked into courtrooms or marches out across the prairie in the dead of winter. Their purpose is to show Adam and Eve before the fall—that we should turn away from materialism and greed. I remember how orthodox Dukhobors used to burn down their houses, torch all their possessions every five years to start fresh, with no attachments to the material world."

"Will, do you believe in God?" I asked.

"Yes, the One within—and maybe Odin, the Vikings' god. In that age man was not made in God's image but gods were made to fit men. Odin had to suffer, give one of his eyes in exchange for wisdom. He had a pair of ravens he sent out every morning to fly around the world. At high noon, they returned to perch on his shoulders, whispering the secrets they had learned. Odin was a god man enough for me."

One day, Malloff and I headed out in the speedboat to Telegraph Cove on a run for supplies when a *williwaw* (a sudden, violent gust of cold land air) roared down a mountain pass, raising waves steep as walls. As we discussed whether to continue or turn around, Malloff broke off in midsentence, slumping forward, hand dropping off the steering wheel, his head rolling over to the side. Without thought, and so fast it seemed slow motion, my left hand grabbed the wheel; I shouted—then watched my right hand slap Malloff across the face.

He lifted his head, deep pain pinching his face, his body shaken by a horrid cough. But he pulled together, turning the boat around.

At first, as we surfed the waves back toward the island, we were silent. Back at the house, we both spoke at the same time.

"What hap–"

"No use hiding it anymore. Michael, I have cancer in my lung—a big tumor. Yeah, it's time to get to work on it. Been puttin' it off too damn long."

After a moment of trying to absorb the shock of those words and the lingering sting in my hand, I said quietly, "Cancer. . . . What do you mean, 'work on it'?"

He looked over into my eyes, and I saw fear and confidence at the same time, as if he were finally accepting a long-offered challenge. "I can get rid of it myself."

"How?"

He took his pipe and tobacco pouch out of his coat pocket, opened the side window, and flung them into a breaking wave. "Quit suckin' on that, for starters. . . . And I have a technique for burning it away."

"I don't understand. What do you mean?"

"I use a power—energy from within."

I was skeptical, feeling that an inner sickness required an "outside" cure—a doctor and drugs. And if the disease was as grave as cancer, the more outside help one would need. However, in Will Malloff's case I kept an open mind. Having lived as an "outsider" most of his life, I knew Malloff had traveled far beyond the norms of society. He was an explorer whose maps I wanted to study.

The next morning we were back at work milling lumber. I watched Malloff closely, told him to take it easy. But he kept up a quick pace. Then, each afternoon after that, for an hour or so he went off by himself in the house or into the woods. Once, when I was returning from fishing, he stepped out of the forest looking totally spent.

"You all right?"

"Yes—but it takes everything I have."

That night after dinner, I tried to pin him down on exactly what he was doing. I asked if it was like the force that, when you hold a magnifying glass out to the sun, concentrating all the rays into one spot, burns through what you hold before it. "Yes, but to get rid of cancer," he answered, "you need to create a laser—a lot of energy focused together—an intense beam to burn away the growth."

In just a few months, the tumor was completely cleared. Malloff checked it on the chest-scanner at a Vancouver hospital.

As a young boy, while watching a traveling hypnotist perform inside a big tent, Malloff instinctively knew everything the man was doing. One of Malloff's earliest cases was a neighbor girl he cured of stuttering. But then, having taken her problem away, Malloff himself stuttered for a few days.

Many nights, deep in island solitude, we sat at the

table in a ring of kerosene lamps, talking for hours about the powers of the mind. I felt like Gurdjieff in his *Meetings with Remarkable Men*—only Will Malloff was all the mystics rolled into one. Once, Malloff hypnotized me to demonstrate mental force. To start with, there was no swinging watch or pendulum—he simply had me concentrate on a nail hole in the wall as he spoke in a calm voice. My eyes remained open. I was carried along on the smooth current of his voice, the nail hole expanding as wide as a lake around me.

Whenever Malloff flicked a big finger out at me, that motion would instantly bring me back—or the same motion repeated would return me, instantaneously, to the deep level of hypnosis. Once Malloff was sure I was comfortable, totally relaxed—he told me that he was going to place a hot butter knife on top of my forearm. He reached over, extending the blade. I felt it touch—then the finger flashed. When I was again fully conscious, he told me to grab the knife. It was stone cold, and had been all the while. But there on my arm was a small burn blister: physical proof of the power of suggestion.

"That's what our minds can do to us," Malloff said. "Negative thoughts set up diseases. Positive thinking helps increase our strengths. Man's salvation is not in technology—in cold machines—but in the living warmth and power of his energy within."

Malloff talked in detail about the autonomic nervous system: our dormant "Superman" that rises up in times of dire emergency, as when a woman lifts a car off her child after an accident. When I asked why we can't live at that level, he said we would quickly burn out, that it's there as a safeguard, a reservoir of unlimited power for us to tap into.

One day, I was chainsawing a log above the beach, then carrying the firewood rounds up to the house, two at a time, by the handles of hatchets struck into the top of each section. As I was walking back, unloaded, Malloff said, "Stiff neck—left side, eh? Upper cervical is out and I'll bet your right leg is shorter than the left." We went into the house; he told me to lay facedown on the floor. He knelt down, picking up my ankles: "Relax—loosen your legs." He shook them in slow waves, then set them down to measure. "Yep—right leg is short by an inch. You have"—*crunch*—"had a crimp right here," he said with a quick press of the heel of his hand into my lower back.

"Now, let's get the neck." I sat in a chair and lowered my head into his huge hands. As he slowly twisted my head from side to side, feeling for the groove, I tightened, feeling frightening strength. "Let go," he said. It sounded like splintering wood as adhesions broke down; the disk popped back into place.

From then on, once a week, Malloff adjusted me. Strange, lifting a straight head to see blue ocean around the chiropractor's "office." And I wasn't the only patient. Loggers and fishermen arrived unannounced, limping, bent over, up the beach. "Dr." Malloff pushed away the breakfast dishes, stretching them out on the big table—or, for the immense Paul Bunyan types, placed them strategically out across the floor for one quick, decisive adjustment. They bounded away back to work, heads, once again, pointing true north. There were no official office hours, there was no advertising (other than word of mouth), and the fee was on a sliding scale, the patients bringing everything from a fresh-caught king salmon to homemade beer.

Malloff's chiropractic roots began deep in the north woods. As a young man, while working as a faller for a logging company, Malloff was one day clobbered on the head by a "widow maker" (a dead limb). He came to in a hospital, but nothing could be done to cure his constant headache and nausea. If he turned his head, he passed out.

He went to the Mayo Clinic for extensive tests, but nothing showed up on the machines. As a last-ditch effort, the doctors extracted the fluid from around his brain for analysis, causing excruciating pain, the brain being now without its cushion. But nothing was amiss. Afterward, while out walking the streets, feeling like throwing himself in front of the traffic, Malloff stopped in front of a chiropractor's office and stepped in. He waited his turn. When Malloff's name was called, the chiropractor looked up: "My God! Sit down and don't move. . . ."

The doctor made a quick, sure adjustment. Malloff could then actually turn his head slightly to each side. "Son, you are about an eighth of an inch away from death," the chiropractor said. "Your neck is in the 'hangman's position.' " The blow of the heavy limb had twisted Will's vertebrae over, pressing bone against spinal cord.

The chiropractor said it would take months, working every day, to bring Malloff around. He offered the young woodsman a room in his house to stay and made him feel part of his family. In between treatments, Malloff read through the library of thick chiropractic texts and watched the doctor, learning the methods. Once his neck was corrected, health fully restored, Malloff went to the Palmer School of Chiropractic and took formal courses. "As part of the final exam you had to be able to find one human hair inside four layers of newspaper—not only where it was but how long and in what direction it ran," Malloff said. "That's how sharp you had to be before they'd let you touch a spine. I used to take a pumice stone to my fingertips—to always have new, sensitive skin. But now I don't need my hands to diagnose—do it just by looking.

"We were meant to heal our own bodies—the power is there if we stay within ourselves—but all this overeducation, specialization, has taken man far away from his true purpose. The difference with me is that I stayed dumb enough not to ever have known 'better.' "

But as with every human powerhouse I have known, the strengths are countered by a matching weakness, deeply rooted. On a peaceful, isolated island, Malloff was addicted to stress. He couldn't function unless he was under pressure: bill collectors' howling, and cancer—the ultimate deadline to fight.

Malloff was hooked on the pipe: he couldn't master tobacco with its inherent evils. Soon after Malloff cleared his lungs of cancer, the Old Chum cans, the empties, started piling up again in the shop. One day, at the round table, looking across a mound of bills and the real possibility of the bank foreclosing on the island, Malloff smiled. "You know, it's a high, this kind of fight!"

Malloff built his dories the same way—under stress. Inside the shop, the dory bottom sat up on low blocks with a big post wedged in tight between shop ceiling and the dory floor. That way, Malloff had resistance to work against, as he bent the cedar lapstrake planks around, like long bows, from stern to bow, nailing the inner edges to the ribs. After the last plank was in place, Malloff took a sledgehammer and pounded at the big vertical wedge. As it kicked out, there was a sound like a high note struck on a violin as the dory sprang to life, flexed tense all around.

After a long trip to Vancouver, Malloff returned with a beautiful young "Viking" woman named Beth Erickson. When they arrived on the beach, and after greeting Beth, I was about to kick rocks over Malloff's feet for fear the big man would float away. I had never seen him so happy. I caught his eyes. He nodded and a laugh rumbled down deep, then cast off weight as it lilted up with all the lightness and hope of Noah's dove.

Beth had been working as a photographer in Vancouver's CTV studio, taking promotion stills of the likes of Oscar Peterson, Cleo Lane, Count Basie, and Tony Bennett for *TV Guide*. One afternoon, while standing in line for lunch at the Kitsilano Café, she felt a powerful presence behind her. "I turned around and there was this huge man with a big smile on his face. 'Why so happy?' I asked him. He said, 'I live in paradise!' "

Beth had never heard that one before, but then she had never met a man like Malloff. The courtship was swift. Malloff didn't dally with a slow and cautious approach. It was more like: "Me Tarzan, you Jane, and now for the jungle!"

One morning, Beth asked me if I would show her how to jig for cod. We went out over the red snapper hole that Malloff had shown me. We nicknamed the hole "the Refrigerator," for the deep water kept the fish cold and fresh, and in that particular spot, the plentiful snappers were as easy to procure as opening a refrigerator door and pulling one out.

I tied identical lead-weight lures on our hand lines and we tossed them overboard. I caught one snapper, another, then one more. Since Beth didn't have a fish, I suggested that we switch sides. I pulled in two more from her side. She stomped her foot and asked what she was doing wrong. I told her that she was doing everything fine, but that the feel, the touch on the deep lure takes time.

The following morning I heard: "*Haay Michael!*" The dory was on the beach. I went down. A big smile beamed between the two red snappers Beth held up.

It was tremendous to see a person develop so quickly in so many new areas. Malloff and his island world were so vast and different that they would either totally overwhelm you or accelerate your own powers—if you had the same great reach within. Beth welcomed the new challenges. She thrived on trying her strengths, stretching her talents out beyond their limits.

The island environment worked wonders on the city girl. The fresh air, pure water and food—all went into transforming Beth. Like Malloff and me before her, Beth removed her wristwatch. The tides, the swing of the sun and moon, slowed her down to their even pace. Urban tension left her face. Her softened features, along with her confidence, brought out all her beauty.

One afternoon, while I was splitting wood alongside the house, I looked in through a side window at Beth. She wore a sailor jersey, jeans, and an empty knife sheath over her hip. She was slicing a fish she had just caught. A deft hand dropped meaty chunks into the wok, which was set down within the rim of the airtight stove. Beth was humming "Sweet Dreams" and looked so peacefully happy in that primitive galley that she stirred up a line from Kerouac: ". . . a friendly and sensitive human being gal who don't give a shit for martinis every night and all that dumb white machinery in the kitchen."

The distant neighbors started coming by to meet Malloff's new woman, and all were charmed. While putting together spur-of-the-moment feasts, Beth encouraged the fishermen's, loggers', Indians' stories and subtly picked their brains for practical north-woods expertise. She told the tale of how she met Malloff. Malloff proudly informed them of Beth's adjustment to the island. "She's a helluva lot more than a pretty face," said Alec Stuart, our closest neighbor.

Now with a savvy young woman in place in paradise, Malloff searched for a way to make big money. Slow, steady effort like salmon fishing, though very lucrative, didn't fit Malloff's rhythm. He worked in spurts, and it was as if once he mastered something he lost interest—specializing, he grew bored, always needing a new challenge. "Next phase!"

was a phrase he said constantly. "Just like the moon—have to go through all the phases to be full," he remarked one night.

Swinging a couple of loans in Vancouver, he was able to buy a big boat—a thirty-five-foot hulk with an 853-horsepower engine. "A workboat to haul freight, maybe dynamite up past Tremble Island through the uncharted inlet to a big logging camp in at the head. I'll set up a regular run. This is it—the way to go. Going to see the foreman this week about a contract."

But that plan died a sudden death. With the bunk-house full of guests, Malloff stormed in early one morning. "Michael—the boat—it's burning!"

We all jumped up and began running down to the beach. I couldn't believe my eyes: Malloff's hope for steady income warped, twisted over into a platform of fire on the water. The acrid stench of burning fiberglass drove us all into the house where we sat stunned, silently watching the flames burn down. Tears wet Malloff's face. Beth kept her arms around him. . . . Just the night before we had gone over to visit a neighbor. Malloff had lit the stove to take the dampness out of the boat's cabin, forgot to turn it off after we docked. All night a fierce wind blew. . . .

As I sat watching the flames, I recalled what Malloff had told me back in the beginning: "It's paradise here, but watch out—in the next minute it'll try to kill you."

Malloff's true wealth was in his friends. Moving through all levels of life, he attracted a vast mixture of people. At any given time, gathered around the table might be the chief surgeon and administrator of Vancouver General, a Kwakiutl fisherman, a television producer, a kayaker, a corporate lawyer, a folk musician, an orchid expert, or a helicopter pilot. Malloff had room within his persona for all of them and always more. "Have to have the energy," Malloff told me once. "Doesn't matter what they do, as long as they're operating full-bore." His friends would never allow Malloff to go broke. There was always a building project for him to do, a seminar on woodworking to teach. . . .

Peter, the helicopter pilot, was one of Malloff's favorites. We never knew when he'd drop in. He flew a Gazelle—a French-made jet helicopter that landed about five seconds before the sound wave arrived. He'd set it down in the garden, straddling the tomato plants, then step in for a cup of tea. He kept busy taking logging company executives timber cruising, and offered a rapid taxi for those who could afford the steep fare. In between jobs—if he was within a hundred-mile radius—Peter zoomed down to say hello or to drop off a six-pack of beer he picked up in Vancouver a few hours ago.

One day he took Malloff, Beth, and me for a spin. Strange, to step from the primitive island up into a high-tech womb of complex gauges, blinking lights, then the building whine of jet power as we suddenly lifted, swinging clear of the trees. Peter shot us straight up, thousands of feet up, the wide ocean washing in below. The islands—small dots as the Inside Passage shrank—tightened under us. We could see over the white peaks on Vancouver Island out to the far west coast and to a curved, open ocean horizon. Then the rising elevator stopped, paused a moment in midair, then slanted down to the right, dropping, shaggy points of firs rushing up at us. Peter leveled off, then charged ahead, swerving from side to side as he copied the Swanson Island shoreline. I looked out the clear bubble at bald eagles in treetop nests, flapping wings, mouths open in silent screams. We then shot out over Blackfish Sound, dropping down, the ocean heaving closer and closer. I was about to protest when I felt a jolt. Peter had set us down atop a tiny rock pile; each leg strut on the aircraft had independent shocks, allowing us to perch unevenly. With its "pond" rippling all around, this dragonfly rested a moment, then quickly sped away, swinging up sideways, straightening on a high level, then falling down off the edge as Peter gave us a roller-coaster feeling, swooping at 180 miles per hour on two commercial fishing boats tied together in Freshwater Bay and rattling their masts with the blast of our sound. We rode the momentum up a steep curve; then, at the very top, just when the helicopter started to fall backward, Peter kicked in the power, nailing us to the sky with our knees up above our heads. I looked down— or so I thought. The sea and sky must have switched places. . . . The chopper then swiveled and dove. Peter dropped us off on the beach, waved, and shot away.

As we walked slowly, unsteadily toward the house, we had to refocus, suddenly being back in our little niche after the far-flung flight. That initial ride opened up my vision of the Inside Passage. From then on, with my mind's eye, I could look simultaneously from all directions and heights.

The contrast between whirling technology and primitive island was evident, almost absurdly so. One day we spent the morning up in the jet helicopter; after we'd gone to bed that night, at two A.M., Malloff and I had to walk through moonlight into the woods, squeezing off alternate shotgun blasts into the air to be able to get to sleep—a howling wolf pack had insisted on encircling the clearing, exhausting the dogs. But when the guns cut in, the wolves ran off and silence returned.

So angry at all the noise, we both had charged out stark naked. But it felt good, the cold pulling blood to the skin. As we moved under the trees, through the shadows, I looked over at big Will Malloff. We were Ug and Mug, a pair of Neanderthals trundling home from the hunt. The way Malloff was holding his gun—the wooden stock a thick club in his hand—and with his high forehead, deep-set eyes, and powerful body, I saw that, measured by *manna*, the force of life, he would have been the alpha-male—the chief leading the way, blazing the trail.

Kenneth Brower, in *The Starship and The Canoe,* a dual biography of Freeman and George Dyson, wrote about Freeman meeting Will Malloff on Swanson Island. Besides being an astrophysicist at Princeton's Institute for Advanced Studies, Dr. Dyson helped design NASA's space program and was the main consultant for the film *2001: A Space Odyssey.* After taking in Malloff's isolated colony and seeing the wide array of tools, machinery, and piles of old scrap metal from which Malloff repaired or invented a tool to fit any occasion, Freeman said: "It's men like yourself that I'm interested in getting into space."

Malloff thought that over for a while, then said, "I'll go only if I can take my Vise-Grips!"

What a projection, a culmination of all there is to Malloff—to have the hypnotist, boat builder, chiropractor, blacksmith blasting through space, stopping to pinch a star, forge the raw materials for a brave new world.

3

SPRING AWAKENING

The pounding rain slowed to a gentle drizzle. Big winds diminished to breezes, with fir trees brushing a tart fragrance on the wafting air. The budding alder grove was solid bird song. Foxglove, poppies, calypso orchids were pollinated by acrobatic bees. Newborn deer, eagles, whales trailed behind instructive parents.

The sea changed from gray to vibrant green. The chain of life returned one link at a time. Under the warming sun, in the ocean's upper levels, the amoebas were absorbed by diatoms or plankton. The arrow worms, comb jellies, emphausid shrimp drifted in the currents, feeding the herring, which were eaten by the salmon, which were gobbled by seals, which succumbed to killer whales.

One afternoon, I heard rain pelting the sea. I looked up into bright sunshine—but the sound of rain persisted. I held out my hand—it remained dry. I closed my eyes to further open my ears. The sound was coming from behind Flower Island. I thought it might be a spot shower, but there wasn't a cloud in the sky.

I rowed out in the dinghy to investigate. Far ahead, the flat sea was dimpled and ringed as if from rain—but no drops from the sky.

As I swung behind Flower Island, I saw that the Sound was bursting with life. A vast multitude of small fish were breaking the surface, *plip plop plonk*. A herring rain.

The school had its followers. Salmon attacked the herring from underneath. On the surface, gangs of sea gulls seized the leapers. Bald eagles cruised down from seaside perches and snatched the fish, one in each taloned fist. Seals and sea lions worked the outer edges, having a field day. A pod of killer whales arrived on the scene. The big marauders paused, as if undecided about what to eat first.

This rower also got in on the action. I slammed the water with an oar and scooped up a half dozen stunned herring. Twenty minutes later, they were sizzling in the pan.

Again, I experienced an attitude shift. I had previously regarded the food chain as a remote theory dryly expounded by professors. But after seeing the process link up before my eyes, and then dipping my hands into it, I realized that no matter how man tries to remove himself from the animal world, he does not stand apart, aloof at the center of the circle. Rather, if he is wise, he follows it around and around.

As the sea was planting itself, I tilled the garden soil. Just back from one of their trips, Malloff and Beth walked out into the middle of the half acre. Malloff stopped to pick up a handful of loose soil. The Dukhobor squeezed the earth as if to press it into himself.

"It's ready."

After the vegetable seeds were in, we foraged through the forest for what nature had already produced. We picked nettle tops, fiddlehead ferns, and morel mushrooms. From the mud flats, we dug wild onions, leeks, cattail roots.

My vision vacillated between the macro and the micro. My eyes continually swept the panoramic ocean expanses, but then halted to probe an inch of the forest floor. I read in Peter Farb's *Living Earth* that one teaspoon of temperate soil has five million bacteria, twenty million fungi, one million protozoa, and a quarter billion algae. Under a small microscope, I examined a smattering of each.

I looked in on a drop of sea water and was mesmerized by the vibrant swirl of life. I unraveled pine cones, flowers, feathers. I dissected, poked, plunged into. In taking things apart, I was able to see universal patterns. I learned why the aspects of life differ and how the essence remains the same.

As I studied the Kwakiutl totem poles on nearby islands, I saw the progenitors of "modern" art. Picasso didn't invent it, but gave primitive masks and perspectives different twists.

I saw that Indian art embodies a spirit. Modern art is often the mask with nothing behind it. The Kwakiutl carvers spoke of the Spirit moving through their hands into the wood. The totem poles, whether rotting on far islands or hermetically sealed in city museums, possess power, live on like no other art I have encountered. The carvers imbued the killer whales, thunderbirds, bears, and human faces with a spiritual longevity. To this day, their bold eyes stare into you as you look at them.

On the edge of our clearing was a green orb open to the sky. I stopped at this small pond every spring day to witness a world created anew. Chortling frogs pushed out of the warm earth and sprang into the water. Insects called water boatmen, encased in air bubbles, zipped from surface to bottom to surface again. Long-legged striders skated across the surface on flat feet. Clouds of fleas flickered back and forth above the pond. I discovered a female on the bank with dark dots of eggs on her back, produced by parthenogenesis—the ability to create offspring without fertilization.

I watched the dragonflies mate. The male flew in front of the female and clasped her head with the two claws at the end of his abdomen. She curled the tip of her abdomen under and up to his packet of sperm. She laid her fertilized eggs in the shallow water. Each time she dipped the tip of her long abdomen into the water a tiny egg appeared.

I watched the red-winged blackbirds alight on the swaying cattail tops. When I approached them, the birds lifted simultaneously, their epaulets of red dabbing the air.

One afternoon, a wild boar piglet came to the pond. Malloff had imported a few boars and sows to serve as last-resort survival food. I ducked behind tall grass and spied on the rambunctious youngster we named Samson. He plopped into the shallow end, and with a disk nose scooped earth from the bank into the water, creating a warm mire. Samson proceeded to wallow with wild joy. His movements and sounds recalled what an anthropologist wrote to me from Africa: "The native boy was on his belly in the river mud, completely oblivious to anything but that warm union. There were loud, squelching sounds and guttural grunts as he thrust his twig penis in and out of the mud, in and out of his mother earth."

Strolling in the woods, I marveled at the blooms of lime green tipping the cedar fronds. Up above, shimmering with sunlight, the forest canopy showed green not as a color but as a spectrum of hues. I hooked an arm around a slender young tree, squeezing a dual pulse: my blood and the sap surging up into new growth.

The very air seemed to throb from all of life renewing itself. The arrival of spring eased away the heavy weight of winter. I floated around reciting an Indian saying: "Walk lightly in the spring; Mother Earth is pregnant."

One morning, I was sitting inside the house when a hummingbird zipped through an open window and crashed against the wall. I gingerly picked it up off the floor. No larger than three inches, it had a scintillating red throat, thin transparent wings, a needle beak. Its heart was palpitating. The cat sat at my feet, salivating. . . .

"The jaws are too soon for you, little one," I told the bird.

I offered a security blanket by cupping my fingers lightly over its back. After a few minutes, it lifted its head and tiny feet pressed my palm. I walked out into the orchard and opened my hand. The hummingbird zinged up and away.

I wondered how it had come to the island. It is a mystery to me how hummingbirds fly long distances during migration. Their rapid wingbeats (eighty per second) consume so much energy that they couldn't store sufficient fuel for the long haul.

I asked Basil Ambers how the hummingbird manages its migration, sensing there would be an answer science had never considered. "It's easy," the Kwakiutl replied. "Hummingbird is a hitchhiker. He catches a ride on the back of Eagle."

*   *   *

In the back of my mind, life in the city seemed sterile and predictable compared to this Inside Passage chock-full of new views, total challenges, bold adventure. I leapt out of bed every morning wondering, *What's next—what totally new experience today?* I was expanding in so many directions that in the evening I had to get reacquainted with myself all over again.

The small island was an unlimited world. I was never bored. It was a thrill just walking in the woods, for the aimless jaunts always seemed to lead to discoveries. I was forever learning something new about nature or myself. Both I came to realize as being one and the same. The external world reflects our internal composition: a circulatory system of streams and rivers, a sensitive skin of earth, mountain spines, stones as bones, breathing in the surf, hair on grassy headlands. The Indians regarded the earth as a living entity—a human system on a grand scale. And the resemblance went as far as psychological forces finding release as birds, trees, whales, the weather. As Gary Snyder wrote, "Outwardly, the equivalent of the subconscious is the wilderness."

As I walked, I often thought that if modern man realized that what is "outside" of himself originates within, he would give up his fight to subdue nature, understanding that the result is imprisonment for himself. Man is now his own jailor—carrying keys to locked doors, instead of opening his unlimited mind.

Some days the explorations were a struggle. The two hundred annual inches of rainfall grew thick jungle undergrowth. I was confounded at how the dogs moved through the bush out ahead of me, even though I walked the trails cleared by the blade of Malloff's diesel Caterpillar. The hounds ignored the man-made avenues—too sterile. They preferred to fight through bushes full of smells and things to pursue.

One day I dropped down to their perspective and saw a network of low corridors through the salal walls. Obeying a compulsion to penetrate deeper into the forest, I added the "all fours" to my repertoire of moves. To make my way, I walked, waded, climbed, and now dropped to hands and knees, or in tight spots slithered through on my belly.

As I went further in, I saw cedar trees that had grown immense, nearly as giant as their redwood cousins. Overhead, their broad canopies closed out sunlight, thinning the low entanglement of bushes and vines. The open floor was soft and springy from the buildup of detritus.

The high tree needles and leaves tapered to points that pierced the rain. Water fell in long drops, penetrating deep into mossy beds. Gurgling rivulets of water cut channels through the layered loam.

In dank shadows mushrooms grew like crumpled ears. Rotting logs fed stands of maidenhair ferns. Toadstools puffed up into white balloons. Even the rocks looked as soft and porous as sponges.

The air was rich with decay. The smell wasn't putrid but had a clean yeasty odor that expanded in the lungs. If a human being can indeed live on air, then the "breathetarian" would gain weight by going into the rain forest to inhale his daily manna.

I walked on, wondering if I was the first man to step under these giant trees. And I wouldn't have been at all surprised to see an elf or wood nymph appear, for it had all the elements of an enchanted forest. Moments later, I felt the guard hairs on the back of my neck stiffen like wires. I whirled around—nothing human or animal in sight—but as I moved on I felt certain that something was following, watching me. There were wolves on the island and I was probably treading through their domain. I wasn't afraid, knowing they wouldn't attack, but my uneasiness would have been diminished if I could have seen with my own eyes the eyes that were watching me.

I thought of turning back, but it was as if my legs were stuck in fast-forward. I experienced the feeling of predestination: that the course was already plotted and my job was to follow along.

In the heart of the forest was a swamp with water as brown as tea. The air smelled rotten yellow—infected with sulfur. The few trees were gaunt, twisted scarecrows. Stands of devil's club thrived in the mire, their exorbitant health a testimony to the forces of darkness. Swamps, I quickly decided, deserved their evil reputations. The place was repulsive and threatening—as if your worst fear was materializing in the bubbling caldron to suddenly burst out at you. But that's nonsense, I reassured myself, the product of too many late-night horror movies.

I knew I had to continue on, that I was close but not yet there, at the source of my search. I probed the depths of the dark water with a stick and then stepped in. The thick silence was stirred by the suck of muck on rubber boots. My attention was cast down, directing steps. When I raised my head, I saw a phantom that stopped me in my tracks. Here was the pulsing magneto: the soul of an ancient cedar standing oblivious to the mire, made all the more beautiful by it—a serene pillar thirty feet tall, with ocher, cerise, and auburn grain that flowed in long strands, all spiraling together, singing pure tones.

I moved to it. I was surprised at what met my fingertips. From afar it looked as solid as marble, but under the touch, the column was papery soft. The outer tree had eroded, exposing its essence—pith in water, with the pump long past its prime. I sensed that with one push the dry fossil would topple. Roots had dissolved, yet it still knew life. It wore a wild crown of tresses: young cedars sprouting on top, finding sustenance within the grandmother.

I returned often to the swamp, standing in the dark water to watch, absorb the glowing core.

4

ISLAND ANIMALS

In Rhodesia, a pack of Ridgeback dogs, after draining a lion on the run, encircled the great cat in a wheeling hoop of death. On its last stand, the lion whipped its head around to anticipate attack. Triggered by the flash of exposed throat, one dog shot in—teeth snapping through the king of the jungle's jugular vein.

Malloff had brought a male and female Ridgeback to the island to protect his domestic stock from marauding cougars, wolves, and bears. When the pair bred, Malloff sold the Ridgeback litters to homesteaders, loggers, fishermen. With the birth of Cottonwood, Will kept the son and shipped out the father. Cottonwood was a Ridgeback supreme.

His short-haired, golden hide was stretched taut over slabs of muscle. Topping his broad back was the distinctive ridge of hair running contrary to the coat that gave the breed its name. He had a wide head that tapered into a short snout, beady brown eyes, forehead fur that wrinkled when he had things to sort out. No two hands ever enclosed his bull neck. He had teeth to rival a wolf's, and, weighing over a hundred pounds, he could move sideways as fast as forward.

On a full moon night, inside the cabin, Cottonwood and his aged mother were wrapped around the stove, snoring. No denying ancestry—they always sought out the closest thing to Rhodesian heat. Suddenly, Cottonwood jumped up and nearly smashed through the door. Malloff leapt up from the table to get the door out of the dog's way. Cottonwood charged down to the beach and collided with a cougar that had just swum up out of the sea. Malloff shouldered his rifle, but the scope's cross-hairs couldn't divide cat from dog.

Finally, the cougar burst away into the woods. Cottonwood suffered deep gashes across his chest and a torn ear, but he came away from the battle full of confidence. Alone, he had tangled with the lion of the north and lived.

Like a true hunter, Cottonwood took on the characteristics of his prey. He often assumed the lordly pose of chest to the earth, back legs gathered under, front legs extended, head held high. While testing the mettle of visiting dogs, he reared up on hind legs and boxed with front paws. Lying prone in the sun, the hound's hide seemed to radiate golden light.

Stretched out on his side, he seemed to absorb energy from the earth, as if his cells were recharging on a positive ground. He slept soundly—but whenever a visitor started off into the woods, Cottonwood instantly appeared at his or her side, as if feeling personally responsible for anyone entering his domain, offering his sensitive nose as radar to pinpoint the slightest hint of danger.

The dog had remarkable control over a large range of

emotions. One moment he was fangs-bared, fighting fu ,
and the next, visiting children were riding him, using his
ears as a bridle. He was proof of the African adage: "Sure
of his strength, the strongest is therefore gentle."

Cottonwood and I spent many hours wrestling together. I played his nemesis—a big cat in pose and might—
and he welcomed the ruse. We fought controlled wars out
in the middle of the grassy "savanna." We trusted one
another enough to box each other's ears, toss the other end
over end, and chomp limbs that lingered too long. When I
managed to pin him to the ground with my chest and arms,
I felt a tremendous upsurge of power as he battled to break
my hold. I had eighty pounds over the dog in weight, but
in close our strength was evenly matched.

Cottonwood enjoyed our tussles, for they kept him in
top shape, and gave him a chance to work out new moves
he might later use against cougars, wolves, bears. If I had
forgotten to be his lion for a while, he would grab my
"paw" in his teeth and lead me out to our arena.

Cottonwood kept me on my toes by knocking me down.
We played a game, an exercise in awareness called
"Gotcha!" Each tried to sneak up on the other, like a stalk-
ing cougar, to deliver a surprise attack. While I was walking across the clearing with my awareness low, Cottonwood
once came galloping full-tilt from my blind side, slamming
through my legs with his broad chest. He hit like a line-
backer. After he bowled me over, I kept my senses alert at
all times. The dog trained the man well.

Cottonwood had one vice, and that was running deer.
Occasionally, he would slip away into the woods and return the next day dead on his feet. Malloff gave him a
verbal lashing, holding back the first degree until he saw
evidence. When Malloff found a dead doe with Cottonwood's mark, he cut off a chunk of meat and tied it firmly

around his dog's neck. Two warm days later, the hound's pleading howls shattered the island nirvana. Malloff cut away the rotten meat—and Cottonwood was cured.

The dogs' diet consisted mainly of beef bones that Malloff would bring in from the Alert Bay butcher. We kept the crates in the cool storehouse and tossed Cottonwood and his mother a dozen bones a day. They gnawed off the shreds of meat, then cracked open the bones to get at the succulent marrow. Offshore boaters, upon seeing the litter of shanks, scapulas, and ribs, remarked that, at first sight, the island appeared inhabited by cannibals.

Whenever a wolf pack closed in around the clearing, sleep was destroyed by their howls—eerie music that played up and down the spine. Cottonwood would be off and running, rolling in mud to kill his scent, barking everywhere at once to convince the wolves they were up against a matching pack of Ridgebacks. He would repeatedly dash back to check on his arthritic mother, who would be barking backup artillery. If the wolves seemed determined to stay, Malloff and I would come out with shotguns and fire blasts into the air, driving them off.

After one particularly intense howl, the next morning, out in the woods Malloff found a wolf lying in a pool of blood. It bore Cottonwood's mark: one small hole in the throat where the Ridgeback's fang sliced the jugular.

Watching Cottonwood was seeing an animal at full power. The dog's muscles rippled from prowling the woods and swimming island to island. His senses were keen from constantly being tested. Cottonwood had a proud bearing and a perennial gleam in his eyes: his run was the wilderness, instead of city confinement.

Tuffy, the cat, came to the island in exchange for a Ridgeback pup. Right from the start, he was Cottonwood's kitty. The big bruiser gingerly carried tiny Tuff around in his mouth. At night, Malloff had to retrieve the kitten from the doghouse lest he freeze from his pal's slobber.

Many an hour Tuffy stretched out across my chest as I lay back reading or thinking. We matched breaths and he purred an even rattle. Our eyes looked into each other's for long moments. There was a connection—a bridge of *anima*, soul. Staring into him, I pondered Teilhard de Chardin's remark: "The animal knows, of course. But it doesn't know that it knows."

Tuff accepted handouts of seafood, but he was his own provider. He lurked in the tall grass around the garden, eyes darting to the flitting birds. A pet no longer, he slunk low to the ground, muscles bunched like springs. Exploding into the air, he batted at birds with hooks and jabs too fast to follow.

One sunny afternoon, Tuffy was lying on top of a drift-wood log with a paw curled over his eyes, his sides slowly rising and falling. High above, a hovering speck dropped as a feathered anvil. Just as I opened my mouth to shout, the cat sprang six feet straight up and rolled over on his back, claws raking the breast of a hawk. Tuff made a four-point landing on the beach and bolted flat-out under the house. Wings swished sand. The hawk struggled to regain its composure as it flapped away.

I thought of how easy it is in the wild to be lulled by a pleasant sensation, to lower the guard for total abandonment, but in that moment of sensual surrender the lurking hunter strikes. The deer is taken when it tarries at the cool stream, the rabbit is snuffed when it closes out all but the taste of sweet grass . . . the cat is snatched when offering itself to the sun.

In Kwakiutl mythology, the Raven stole the sun. Eagle took it away and put it back up in the sky. True to the myth, our resident raven was a rascal of the first degree.

Like Shakespeare's fool, Blackie was a conniver, prophet, and thespian of unlimited roles.

Whenever I tossed fat scraps to the chickens, Blackie flew the shadows and perched unseen in a nearby tree. The chickens had a warning call, a high-pitched cackle that roughly translated as "Red alert—hawk attack!" Blackie opened his beak and out came the very shriek. With the chickens dashing for cover, the raven swooped down, grabbed up the delectable fat, and flew off—*tok tok tok*—his laughter ringing through the cold air.

The ventriloquist had fun with big, tough Cottonwood. In the thick of the forest, the raven barked like a dog. Cotton ran himself ragged searching for the invader.

Ravens have killed loggers in the woods by imitating the whistles that served as signals. The man operating the donkey engine would hear one short whistle, meaning "go ahead," and he would—pulling in cable. The unsuspecting worker on the other end would be pulverized by the speeding log.

Malloff estimated Blackie to be about fifty years old. Swanson Island's crown was logged in the 1920s, and that may have been when the raven learned his whistles. Whenever Malloff or I started up the chainsaw, Blackie flew over, issuing shrill commands.

Of all the northern birds, ravens are the best fliers. The eagle, with its six-foot wingspan, is an awesome glider, but for sheer maneuverability the raven is unmatched. We would be treated to acrobatic shows after the rains, when the ravens went up above our clearing to air out their wings. Like the Blue Angels jet plane show, Blackie and his mate, in unison, would execute a series of barrel rolls, tumbles, and loop-the-loops. Then the larger male would swerve onto his back, sailing upside down beneath the female. Blackie somehow would hold the position, then snap upright, and he and his mate would side-slip together through the air, then parting to top off the show with a grand finale. From opposite directions, the two ravens would speed directly toward each other. In the last inch of air, simultaneously, the mate would flip onto her back with Blackie vaulting over her.

I once saw Blackie protect the chickens from their feared enemy. The raven handled the diving hawk the way a matador taunts a bull. In midair, Blackie worked his wings like a cape in the raptor's face, leaving it totally exasperated.

A Kwakiutl told me that if you are hunting and see a raven circling, it could be a sign of game below. The raven makes the connection between man's kill and a meal of the discarded guts.

One afternoon, while a visiting lady and I were engaged in a bout of *amore* out on a pine-needle bed, we heard the whir of wings. I rolled over to see Blackie hovering over us, halting our ardor. I reassured the city girl that, no, the big black bird wouldn't attack. We tried to carry on, but the raven sat on a branch directly above us—*kowulkulkulk*—laughing in five syllables.

There I was, deep in the forest, locked limb to limb with a woman—an endangered species in the North—while a damn common raven was not only being a voyeur, but was ridiculing me as well! I felt my desire, *ahem,* shrink away. . . .

I shook a fist at Blackie and cursed: "Quoth the Raven, 'Nevermore'!"

Malloff planted Russian wild boars on the island, and four soon became forty. He affectionately referred to Boris, Ivan, Katarina, and Natasha as "my black flowers." At first we were worried about Ivan the Terrible. We thought he might be gay. He seemed more fond of beautiful Boris, but after observing the big boar in action enough times, Ivan got the hang of it and went on to sire fine litters of his own.

The sows always came into heat during the full moon, and it was a violent coupling. Before Boris drove Ivan off, both boars bred the same female. One bit the sow's ear while the other mounted her, thrusting a corkscrew cock. If one boar stayed aboard too long, the other mercilessly chomped the humper's testicles, then hopped on for his turn. The disposed boar then turned to the battered ear, grunting hot messages between bites.

Their ferocious lust lasted for hours. When the sow's front legs caved in, the thrusting boars drove her forward, her knees plowing furrows in the earth. They were oblivious to anything beyond their immediate nerve endings. The ménage à trois bounced off the buildings and crashed through the bush, heaving and squealing, driven by the instinct that demands propagation.

The pigs had roam of the entire island. Everywhere we hiked, we saw their cloven hoofprints and overturned soil with snipped roots. I was concerned that the cougar would dine on suckling pig, but the adult boars kept all threats at bay.

Wild boars are extremely dangerous when cornered. While exploring, I moved through the bush with all senses on the alert. Boris and Ivan were sprouting wicked tusks that curled out from lower jaws. I knew the power and leverage of those fangs from a tug-of-war I had with Ivan in the clearing. He shredded a fish-scented towel with a shake of his head.

One night, I saw exactly how a mother sow attacks when she and her young are cornered. Inside the cabin, Cottonwood and his mom were wrapped around the stove, snoring away. When I later sent them out for the night, the groggy pair sauntered over to their doghouse. Cottonwood suddenly exploded into rage. A mother sow and her four piglets had taken up residence inside the dogs' domain. Cottonwood charged in—then jumped backward, barely escaping gnashing jaws. Inside the dark hut, a pair of blood-red eyes glowered like hot coals.

I called Cottonwood off, not wanting him to misjudge the sow's maternal instinct. I formulated a quick plan, grabbed a rear corner of the doghouse, and heaved. The pigs all poured out, dashing helter-skelter across the clearing. Squeals of agony pierced the night as Cottonwood chomped fleeing hams.

Malloff brought the boars to the island mainly to create meadows. By selective logging, he had opened up patches of ground to the sun, and the plan was for the pigs to clean out the roots and aerate the soil for wheat and grass, which would, in turn, support a future herd of Highland cattle.

Always trying to ensure privacy, Malloff also hoped that the boars would scare off unwanted visitors or prod friends slow to leave. During severe cold spells we had tossed the porkers handouts of fish heads and beef bones. Pigs remember with their stomachs. From then on they came to us whenever we called, *"Here, pig-pig-pigeees! Soooeeee pigs!"*

For the uninitiated visitor, it was an overwhelming sight to see a gang of wild boars come charging out of the woods, salivating as they converged around you!

One morning I left with friends to visit Mammallilacoola, an old abandoned Kwakiutl village on a nearby island. We would only be gone half the day, so I didn't bother to lock the doors.

When we returned, I walked back to the storeroom to put away a share of the berries we had picked. The dogs, instead of jumping all over me upon my return, were acting tense and agitated. Coming out of the storeroom, I saw why—the back door of the house was half open. At first, I thought the hounds were feeling guilty for having nosed the door open, but when I squatted down to look them in the eyes, they didn't hang their heads or nervously yawn. Just the opposite—Cottonwood's ridge bristled up, signaling that we had a serious matter to deal with. I tiptoed across the porch and looked inside the house. My heart fell into my boots. It was the ending of *Animal Farm*.

Containers of food, books, clothes, typing paper, and pillows lay mashed and shredded on the floor. Furniture was toppled. There was a plop of dung on my crashed typewriter!

Ivan was standing up on the bench looking at himself in the mirror. The sows were stretched out across the daybed. The piglets were snoozing on beds of scattered rice. Boris was hunkered down on a throw rug with his head half buried in a bucket of raisins.

I stamped my foot. Together, all heads snapped up. Boris gave a startled grunt. The sows shrieked with anticipated pain. "Hee—*outahere*!" I blasted.

They scrambled to their feet and careened off each other as their stubby legs slip-slid over the linoleum floor. I didn't open the side door to let them out easy, and even though the wild boars had their backs to the walls, my anger overpowered my fear. They all poured out the only exit into a gauntlet of kicking boots and Ridgeback fangs.

On cold nights the pigs piled up in a heap under the dory shop. Horrible sounds of mayhem issued forth as they argued over whose turn it was to be the blanket. One evening, inside the shop, a visitor from Vancouver was watching Malloff working on a new dory. When the wailing and gnashing of tusks started up beneath them, all the blood dropped from the man's face. "Wha-what the hell is *that*?"

Without missing a stroke with his spokeshave, Malloff replied, "Pack of Russian wild boars. Oh, forgot to tell you—careful where you step. Weak floorboards here and there."

5

SUMMER VISITORS

Suddenly molten sun blazed across blue sky. There was heat to defeat the dampness of surrounding sea and engulfing rain forest. There was light that dappled the sea with shimmering waves, light that poured like solid pillars through the canopy of trees. The pounds of soggy wool were discarded. Sun on skin was all I wore. Pores opened like blossoms to sip the blazing energy that filled twenty hours of each day. In the North, for the sun I developed an Aztec's regard.

The summer sun seemed to solidify in the sky. Each hour was a day long. By noon, I was as becalmed as the day. The air puffed just enough to lift the nape feathers on perched eagles. I sat up in the crook of an old cedar, watching anthropomorphic clouds play charades across the sky.

With Malloff and Beth away on another extended journey, I was once again alone. The most well known island man—Robinson Crusoe—shared my hammock and state of mind. I reread the story with much more understanding since I had met some of his challenges. And like Crusoe, I was not totally alone. Many "Fridays" made their appearances during the summer months when the sea was calm. The island was remote, but it was on the exposed edge of remoteness; therefore, other footprints appeared in the sand.

During my stay, whale consciousness was on the rise. To the cetacean devotee, *Mind in the Waters* became the Book of Revelations, inspiring young people to make pilgrimages to wherever whales are gathered. The book hooks you with a blend of dazzling photographs, fine art, and whale and dolphin articles penned by scientists, mythologists, poets. Dr. Paul Spong, cetologist and one of the founders of Greenpeace, gave a lyrical account of his close encounters with the killer whales of Blackfish Sound. Throughout the summer a procession of "whalies" stopped in at Freshwater Bay asking directions to Spong's camp.

Many were from Los Angeles. An Indian fishing boat would swing into the bay to disgorge a rubber skiff over the side. A pair of eager young men would motor in, their Zodiac inflatable crammed with all-weather clothing, astronaut food, sleek silver cases full of camera gear. I would invite them in for coffee to find out if they were qualified to live up to their intentions and the demands of the country. If they had as much inside of themselves as they did in their Zodiacs, I would then point the way across to Dr. Spong's camp.

One L.A. man kept sniffing and rubbing his nose as he stepped out of his Zodiac onto the beach at Freshwater Bay. I was sure he was high on cocaine.

"What is *that*?" he said after yet another sniff.

"What is what?"

He inhaled so deeply that his chest hit his chin.

"Oh-ho!" I chuckled. "That is one hundred percent air."

"Damn," he said as he did another snort. "L.A.—you know—never breathed *this*!"

During the summer many sailboats and power yachts from West Coast cities meandered up the Inside Passage, some going all the way to Alaska. Many of them temporarily anchored in Freshwater Bay—the last shelter before a stretch of open ocean.

The sailboats slipped quietly in and out. The crews were either singlehanders or young couples, and most had built their boats themselves. The sailors eschewed electronics, weighty gadgets—anything that got between them and what they were out there after. In quest of the marrow, comforts of the flesh were stripped away.

It was a different story with the power yachts. It was as if swank country clubs had been compacted into motorized, seagoing squares. Many of them roared into the bay, bullhorns blasting, *We're here*!

The captains invited me aboard their floating Winnebagos not so much to meet, but to show off the accoutrements: teak-paneled dining room; six-stool, brass-rail bar; wine cellar; TV and wall-of-sound system; deluxe kitchen complete with automatic garbage compactor. One palace had a sunken bathtub; another carried two slot machines. "We always travel with the comforts of home," was the common proclamation.

More than once, while the first mate made coffee, the commander got up, pushed the button to fire the engine, then slid back the hatch cover. I was supposed to be impressed by all that power. One drunk straddled the rumbling metal, waving an unsteady hand over the throttle lever. "*If I crack 'er open, she'll snap your head off!*"

One yacht roared in just as I returned from fishing. It threw a rooster tail that nearly toppled the dory, then stopped dead in the water. Shrill female laughter fell off the bridge. I charged toward the behemoth with profane salvos lined up on my tongue.

"Sorry, Jack, didn't see you from up here." A man's half-crocked face grinned over the rail.

Out of the corner of my eye I caught the license number and couldn't miss the name: F.U.J.I.M.O. was painted in tall letters across the stern.

"What do the initials stand for?" I asked. "Something oriental?"

"No." He laughed. "They mean . . . uh . . . ."

"What?"

"Well, you might not want to hear it just right now."

"Go ahead, try me."

"F.U.J.I.M.O. is short for 'Fuck You, Jack, I'm Movin' Out.'"

I suggested that he do the latter.

The visiting yachtsmen immediately asked about the fishing. "Hear the salmon are really running around here!" was their usual opener.

"They come and go," I would reply.

"What's a guy get 'em with here?"

"Euclata flasher, twenty-seven-inch tail, one pearl, Mustag seven hook, number four hootchie."

"Wanna run that by me again?"

"Oh—just about anything will do."

"No, all those names and numbers."

I would study the eyes and ask a few questions of my own. If I was talking with a fisherman, then I would supply the fine points.

One man I remained evasive with reached into his wallet, plucked out a twenty-dollar bill, and waved it in

68

front of my nose. A maître d' may have given him a table, but this island boy didn't lead him to the fish.

I wondered how the drunk drivers could possibly make it all the way to Alaska, but for the most part the weather was mild and the ocean a wide highway to absorb their weavings. However, nearly every summer the Coast Guard was called out to try to save a half-million-dollar beauty that was smashed on the rocks (cause and effect—identical), or to tow in another party that had pumped gasoline into a diesel engine.

The invasion continued with a fifty-foot, three-tiered yacht that rumbled into the bay one afternoon. I rowed out in the dinghy later that evening to ask if they would turn off their television so I could pull in the marine weather report over the small radio.

There I met Frank—placing him originally from the Midwest, say Milwaukee—lately of L.A. Beefy face, hams for hands, a big-boned body with a keg for a stomach.

"Sure, son." He pressed an intercom button. "Shut that blasted thing off and come up with a couple cold ones." He turned back to me. "Hope you don't mind us tossin' our hook here."

"I've no claim on the water."

"Great place you have." A thick arm swept around in a circle. "Just what a man needs."

From the spiral staircase emerged a nut-brown young woman in a teeny bikini that displayed perfect curves. Under a mane of blond hair glistened turquoise eyes. Full lips formed an inviting smile.

"This here's Bambi. Sorry—didn't get yours. . . ."

I was about to say Rip van Winkle, but stayed with common Michael.

Bambi handed us the beers and then twirled slowly down the steps, while I absorbed each bare, tantalizing plane of "Nude Descending Staircase" through the slats.

Frank and I sucked the brews and yakked about fishing. Then the inevitable: "Come on, Mike, I'll show you around." It was the usual grand tour, but this time far more revealing. Just as we were heading back up to the bridge, he said, "Have a look at this."

Frank unlocked a long closet. It was Abercrombie & Fitch—with all the departments. I looked over a Mann-licker rifle, a matched pair of English shotguns, graphite fishing poles, reels in five sizes, box after box of lures and ammo, fleece-lined hip waders, a rack of safari clothes.

"Spent all my life workin', with never a goddamned day off. Vacations were for everybody else but me. But now I'm gonna make up for it. Sold out the truckin' firm and ditched a naggin' wife. Now I'm a free man. But you know, it's all kinda strange. Never knew how to play and now I gotta learn. Ever hear such a thing in this day and age? All I've ever known is bust-ass work, but now—now I'm gonna play as damn hard as I worked," he announced, catching Bambi around the waist.

"Hey, before you go, what about that fishing . . . ?"

Who could resist? The next day Rip van Winkle showed beefy Frank and beautiful Bambi how to play the salmon.

It has been said that if you stay in one place long enough, all the world will come to you. I found that to be true. Around a solid hub many spokes revolve. By holding together the island center that Malloff established, I wheeled around the earth.

During the summer, Americans, English, Australians, Germans, French, Swedes, and Polynesians paused at Freshwater Bay while experiencing the fabled Inside Passage. Each person brought aboard the island current events and his or her own interesting history. Some days the bay looked like a marina loaded with boats flying all flags. Having gathered the international roamers at the round table, I drew them out with well-placed questions. I listened, I reveled, and traveled the globe.

Having recently emerged from a retreat into solitude, I welcomed people, viewing them with fresh eyes. Any misanthropic feelings I had had were now gone. Each visitor was sharply delineated against the background of my geographical isolation. In vast expanses, people stand out in bold relief.

Many of the visitors were bona fide characters, adventurers through all realms of life. The writer in me got greedy. I kept them up late into the night, wanting to hear more of their lives that later I scribbled down and held as ore to someday shape into sterling novels.

The following morning I would awaken to the sound of their anchor chains clanking up, sails snapping in the wind. An exchange of hand waves, and away they went. Then, just as I finished cleaning the house, another flotilla would arrive to begin a new round of food, talk, drink—fishing and hiking if they weren't in a hurry.

By August, I felt like a stale tour guide. I wanted a stretch of time alone, but then on the distant horizon the dark winter loomed. I remembered. I didn't shun anyone.

On the marine charts, Freshwater Bay was marked as a store. Sixty years ago, it served as a trading post, exchanging groceries for fish and furs. However, after the post faded, the symbol was never deleted from subsequent charts. That tiny merchant mark brought in all sorts of "desperados." They ranged from a singlehander whose perishables were devoured by a stowaway rat to a family wanting sugar so that Mother could sprinkle a topping on the cookies.

The first few times, I explained that the store was long gone, but then—what the hell—I decided to carry on the old trading post tradition. Depending on the volume of my own supplies, I would barter for whatever was needed, quickly learning "frontier economics": it's not intrinsic value that counts, but whether you can supply their demand. It turned out that I held the aces. To boat people, fresh garden vegetables or a head of lettuce were worth triple their weight in hamburger or beer.

A yachting magazine got wind of Freshwater Bay's hospitality to mariners. In an article on friendly harbors, we were mentioned as "the hosts of the coast." But it wasn't all my doing. Malloff had always offered full amenities to the amiable and interesting.

However, the publicity infuriated Malloff. Having rubbed elbows with enough people on business trips in distant cities, upon returning to the island he looked forward to the even flow of uninterrupted work. Instead, many of the magazine's subscribers put Freshwater Bay atop their Inside Passage itineraries.

"I'm going to scout around for a couple cannons," Malloff declared as he headed out in search of peace and quiet. "We'll put one on each side of the house and when a boat shows itself the first ball will round off their mast. If that doesn't make 'em turn tail, they'll take the next shot broadside!"

With cannons pending, twin cream-colored castles motored in late one day. They tied up abreast and dropped their hooks into the bay. I was out on the log raft mending crab traps. We exchanged greetings—but they then kept to themselves. During "happy hour" the foursome sat up on the bridge in their padded chairs. They tossed down Canadian Club as they watched the sun complete its arc. One man kept extending his arm as if orchestrating the colors. One of the women spotted something out at sea.

"Look—is that a whale?"

"Hmmm . . . too far away to tell—but it's definitely something."

"I'll go get the telescope."

The man returned with a Telemaster.

"Well, I'll be. Take a look at this."

Each put an eye to the glass.

"Poor things!"

"Maybe they're Indians."

A two-man kayak, returning from Alaska, glided into the bay. Its occupants, Harry and Jack, worked the paddles like extended arms. Endless days of sun had stained them mahogany. The long haul had brought out an abundance of muscles that shifted under taut skin like steel coils. It was clear, even to the comfortable, that the kayakers had reached and were now returning from a great adventure. The yacht party set down their drinks, stood up, and applauded.

Summer was when Harry Williams, Stuart Marshall, and George Dyson entered their kayaks to ride the tides and winds of the Inside Passage. Harry is a blond, apple-cheeked young man who has explored just about every nook of the convoluted British Columbia coast. His favorite traveling companion was an antique Gibson mandolin upon which he masterfully played a full range of folk songs.

Stuart Marshall was previously a commercial artist in New York City, but the money wasn't worth the imprisonment. He roamed the Northwest coast in a slim cedar kayak, pausing to capture the scenery in dazzling watercolors that museums and private collectors bought as fast as he made.

In a park outside of Vancouver, George Dyson built a treehouse ninety-five feet up in a Douglas fir. Living high in the sky, in retreat, he made great advances in kayak design. In a shop below, he constructed *baidarkas*—the Russians' name for the Aleut Eskimos' big kayaks. But instead of stitching sealskins over a whalebone frame, George used fiberglass over aluminum tubing. His fleet consisted of a family-sized fifty-four-footer with six manholes, and six twenty-eight-footers that carry three people each. Besides being paddled, the baidarkas were built to sail. The twenty-eight-footers easily reached ten knots under a half-moon sail cut from parachute cloth.

George has an artist's knack for giving found objects new life by using them in unexpected forms. One of his creations, to my mind, matches Picasso's genius for juxtaposing a bicycle seat and upraised handlebars into "Head of a Bull." One day, George returned from the Vancouver dump with discarded stop signs. He melted the aluminum octagons down into sleek baidarka paddles, transforming STOP into GO.

George is currently designing a baidarka that will be tethered to a large canvas kite sailing high above. "It will permit one to do two of the most delightful things: skim the surface of the sea and fly a kite at the same time."

George's creations seem far-flung to the mollasses masses. People that encounter a new-age baidarka out at sea are startled, to say the least. The crews of fishing boats and big freighters yell down, "Whatta ya doin out here?"

"Going to Alaska," George replies.

"Ya gotta be crazy!"

George's father, Freeman Dyson, an astrophysicist at Princeton's Institute for Advanced Studies, once wrote, "When the great innovation appears, it will almost certainly be in a muddled, incomplete and confusing form. To the discoverer himself, it will be only half-understood, to everybody else it will be a mystery. For any speculation which at first glance does not look crazy, there is no hope."

During a visit with his dad at the Institute, George showed slides of the baidarka's evolution to an audience of distinguished scientists. Afterward, Margaret Einstein said to him, "Uncle Albert would have been enthralled!"

George, Harry, and Stuart often talked of traveling together, but when the first warm southeaster blew, the free spirits sailed off to different destinations. Occasionally their bows would cross, and they regarded such spontaneous rendezvous as much more meaningful than if planned.

Each packed a wok and a pair of chopsticks. Each trailed a baited hook and knew all the edible greens, land and sea. Like the wild animals around them, they alternated between feast and fast. At night, the kayakers either landed on a beach, folding their sails like tepees around them, or they slid their shells into a kelp patch and slept protected with the sea otters. Through the thin kayak walls, whale reverberations arose from the deep—a sound track to their dreams.

In the quietly gliding kayaks, the men saw animals performing wild rites. Harry was riding the tide alongside an island when he watched in amazement as a wolf brought down a deer. Hungry Harry spooked the wolf, then struck a fire and sat down to a feast of roast venison. While George was camped on an isolated Alaska beach, a Kodiak bear arrived to display his territorial dominance. The giant bruin pushed over trees and flung boulders around like basketballs. George paddled on. . . .

One night, Stuart was stretched out in the bottom of

his kayak, upturned face framed by the open aperture. He was gazing up at the stars, drifting, when suddenly the ocean erupted with a humpback whale breaching up and over the kayak. "Seeing the whale roll across the stars—clear over me—was pure magic!"

The kayakers drew up their own charts showing distances not in miles but in hours paddled. They demarcated soft sleeping beaches, cod holes, clam beds, berry bushes, bird-egg cliffs, hot springs, totem poles, Indian petroglyphs. They dressed like gypsies, talked like pirates. Their buried treasure was a case of Crown Royal that George had stashed in a deep cove—to be dipped into only for emergency barter or ravenous thirst.

The toughest of men, George, Harry, and Stuart weren't afraid to let the boy in them romp free. Like modern-day Huck Finns, each summer they forgot adult obligations to live in quest of adventure and strange happenings.

George was clipping along just south of Ketchikan when he spotted a trimaran tilted against a large rock. He went over to see if the situation was as bad as it looked. George nearly tripped over a man lying spread-eagled on the rock. The startled gent jumped up, profusely embarrassed. He pointed down to the imprint in the rock. The petroglyph of "The Man Who Fell from Heaven" was a perfect fit.

One afternoon, I spotted a baidarka out in Blackfish Sound. It was like looking at a Chinese wash: counterpointing the immense mountains and sea was a tiny half-moon sail pitching like a paper lantern in the wind.

The baidarka swung into the bay and the sail dropped. One double-bladed paddle dipped from side to side. The slender boat slid up onto the sand with a hiss. George Dyson looked up at me, blinking.

"George! Holy hell! Alaska—you made it!"

A smile flickered across his sunburned lips and he shrugged as if to say that Alaska was not the end of the world but just another step in his journey.

He placed swollen hands on the manhole rim and slowly unfolded himself. Ebony torso; baggy, fish-smeared pants; black hightop sneakers with busted laces. His ribs corrugated his chest; his collarbone was a ledge on either side; deep hollows sunk beneath his eyes. In shrinking vast distances, the body had shrunk itself. After food was consumed by the relentless paddle, the body melted fat and burned into muscle. George had traded pounds of flesh for what filled his spirit.

I looked over the baidarka and asked how it had held up. (Alaska was the prime destination of the kayakers that summer, and they had all stopped in on their way north to fine-tune their boats in Malloff's various shops.) George said he was very pleased. A few things to alter, but it had proven stable, hadn't rolled over once, and there had been twelve-foot seas.

I asked if he wanted a bath or maybe rest or how about a meal. He nodded at the latter.

"Just came in with a lingcod—I'll get it going," I said.

He looked off toward the garden. "A salad . . ."

I stood in the doorway and watched him. When George was stationary, his body seemed at odds with itself, the overall picture being interrupted by pronounced edges and angles. But when he started in motion, elbows, protruding ribs, a wayward nose all blended into a synchronized form. George moved with the relaxed smoothness of a wild animal.

He didn't pause in front of the garden fence, didn't climb on it. He flowed over in one motion like a deer.

Harry, too, had an animal within, but one of a different ilk. He contained the wolf. During one of his visits, he took down an old fiddle and bow from the cabin wall and went outside. Harry was just beginning on the fiddle, so the runs were broken up by screeches and wails. Cottonwood ambled over and sat back on his haunches next to Harry. Upon the next screech, the hound lifted his muzzle to the sky and howled. Undaunted, Harry grinned and sawed on. Cottonwood trailed off, but then came in strong at the chorus. Harry shrugged, set the fiddle down, and howled along. Like jam musicians, the psuedo-wolves sat there intertwining wild sounds.

Stuart spent a summer kayaking up Knight's Inlet, where the ocean winds ninety miles into the British Columbia mainland, creating a fjord full of magnificent scenery and unpredictable powers. Mountains with hanging glaciers and fog in their folds tower above the serpentine sea. Colossal waterspouts, whirlpools, and tidal waves are common occurrences. It is a cryptic place—sacred to the Kwakiutls. Stuart spoke of the grizzly bears he encountered while taking side trips up the rivers. He found himself floating directly between gangs of fish-feeding bears lining both sides of the stream. Where the channel narrowed, the bears were only an arm's swipe apart. But being that these bruins lived in isolation, toward man they were far more curious than dangerous. The grizzly gauntlet swung only their heads at the strange apparition that floated by.

Of all the visitors to the island, it was the kayakers I most wanted to see. They extended me, gave me the impetus to put complete trust in nature and my own powers, to challenge myself to live up to full potential, peak performance.

One of George Dyson's dreams is to paddle/sail a baidarka across the Bering Sea—from Alaska to Siberia—a stretch of six hundred hazardous miles.

"All we need is three good days."

"Do you ever fear it?" I asked him.

He shook his head and calmly said: "Two things can happen. We'll either make it or we'll die."

George, Harry, and Stuart have been out on the edge so often that they have flattened it into a trail. Their feeling for the ocean is much like that of the Kwakiutls of old. If wind or wave does you in, it just might be your fault. You may have been living in such a manner that the harmony was broken.

When the kayakers arrived, the writer in me wanted to pull them out of their boats, set them down on the sand, and ply them with questions. But the reportorial style is not well received in the North. In fact, writers are regarded as raccoons: wearing masks and nosing about where they shouldn't. Once when I was reading a passage from *Never Cry Wolf* to a Kwakiutl, he stopped me in mid-sentence and asked who wrote it.

"Farley Mowat," I said.

"Hardly Know-it," he said.

So when the kayakers hit the beach, I held back my questions. They knew that I wanted to know, and in time they spoke of their adventures—always when I was farthest away from pen and paper. But their way made me a better writer. It trained my memory, an instrument that doesn't intrude between scribe and subject.

I also learned that silence can reveal as much if not more than words. I had observed the elder Kwakiutls sitting next to each other for long periods with closed mouths. It wasn't that they didn't have anything to say, but rather they sent their thoughts across the bridge of silence.

A couple days after George arrived from Alaska, he walked out on the beach and faced the wind. "Stuart will be here today," he said. Sure enough, later that afternoon we watched a distant log become a kayak become Stuart in front of us. He emerged naked from the cedar looking so tan and clean and gleaming with health that I felt ashamed to have clothes on. Stuart and George sat cross-legged up on the grass. They were silent for half an hour. When they spoke, it was of future plans.

"Man, these guys are light-years ahead!" said a Los Angeleno, Bill Meredith, who happened to be on the island when the kayakers were coming in from Alaska. Bill's dream was to scuba dive with the killer whales. At first I thought he was another thrill seeker chasing the big high, but as he talked, I learned that his passion was based on deep knowledge. He was a cetacean scholar, devouring every book, article, and film on dolphins and whales. But words and pictures only go so far. Bill came north to see his favorites for himself—the killer whales of Blackfish Sound.

Bill, George, and I were lounging on the "lawn" one afternoon, recovering from a clam feed, when we heard explosions of breath and then saw the tall dagger fins. Bill leapt to his feet; George said, "Let's go!"

We ran the baidarka down to the water. Bill got into the front manhole, George slipped into the stern; I kicked us out and hopped into the midsection. The paddles slashed. The kayak lifted and shot over the water.

Out in the bow of a baidarka you feel like the tip of a hurtled spear. "L.A. Bill" was thrust into the wild.

We kept power stroking, three as one, but the killer whales were intent on traveling. They easily outdistanced us.

As we paddled back to the island, Bill was silent. I sensed not disappointment but the other extreme. When he turned around, his lips moved, but there were no words. I saw from his eyes that he was embedded deep in the excitement I had felt many times.

After dinner that evening, George went off alone. Bill and I went out into the night and sat with our backs against the beached baidarka. The sharpness returned to Bill's eyes. "Today my life changed," he said. When I asked how so, he spoke of George like Kerouac chanting Cassidy. Bill wound down with, ". . . and he's so out there into it all that he makes me feel that I haven't done anything meaningful, that I've taken the easy, secure way out. George shames me, but in the right way. He's into so many dimensions that he makes me want to be there too."

I smiled. "That's just how he and Stuart make me feel. And I was thinking today that it's across cultures. These are young white guys living the old Indian ways. They've tapped into the elemental forces. The powers that modern man has turned away from, they are bringing back to life."

Bill asked about George's treehouse. I told him how George towed in a drifting cedar log and split long shakes; how he used the tree's high branches as integral supports; how instead of nailing, he used miles of thin rope to lash the house together; how it flexed with the swaying fir through a sixty-knot gale; how he went to the dump in search of a picture window.

"He couldn't use the usual square pane," I explained. "It couldn't take the high winds. When he came across an old television screen, he knew that the convex shape would distribute the stress. There he is, high in the sky, dreaming kayaks, writing poetry, planning expeditions—producing inside the screen, instead of watching and rotting!"

For me, George Dyson is a link with our arboreal

past. When our distant ancestors left the trees, they dropped into a world of fang and claw. We were, and still are, so preoccupied with fighting for survival that many of us have lost our perspective—the ability to get above and beyond personal problems to see the big picture. George is still living on high. He sees what is required of man to ensure a future for this planet. His baidarkas may best show us the way.

George had left one of his twenty-eight-foot kayaks on the island for a few months. The baidarka set me free. I became a water bird bobbing over the swells. I perched on rock piles, speared fish, sailed with wings unfurled.

One day, I put on a hooded poncho that George had designed to cinch around the manhole rim, making the kayaker Aleut-impervious to rain and salt spray. I stretched hatch covers over the other two manholes, then paddled out into the teeth of a westerly raking the bay. The waves crashed over the boat and my back. How exhilarating not to have to run from the sea—to be able to take it head-on, slashing through with nothing to lose. When the swells actually became predictable, I turned in a trough and surfed the steep walls home.

I enjoyed paddling out into the fog, especially at night. Seated snug and warm in the narrow baidarka, I knifed smoothly inside the muslin-thick air, my ears fanning out, alert for the rumblings of big freighters, Alaska-bound. At first sound, I raced far from their deepwater path, feeling the huge propeller screws churning underwater, vibrating the taut sides of the kayak. I then waited for the increasing sounds to suddenly materialize.

One night, a fantastic apparition appeared: a phantom seven stories tall—a floating city with every light blazing. It went on and on, an endless white length, a surreal mirage surpassing any dream—seen by a solitary kayaker staring up at hundreds of people, in elegant dress, slow-dancing on the brightly illuminated upper deck.

The ship cruised on, leaving eerie music trapped in the fog:

> "Dreeemzzs come truuuu
> In bluuu Hawai-eeeee . . ."

6

~~~~~~~~~~

SALMON FISHING

During the summer, thousands of tons of chum, coho, sockeye, humpback, and king salmon streamed through Blackfish Sound, with the sea jammed with fishing boats after their shares. Swanson Island was surrounded by an armada of commercial boats working eighteen- to twenty-hour days to haul in a year's harvest in a single season.

I had a ringside seat, watching out the windows as big purse-seiners encircled nets around a massive run. At night, the gill-netters took over, closing off the gaps, the channels between islands, like spiders spinning webs. And out before sunup, running back into sheltered bays at night, were the trollers—solitary or paired men on small boats with outrigger wings, tirelessly towing lures back and forth, high and low, day after day barely making wages—then in a three-day streak hooking $30,000 worth of big kings.

Unlike the sixty-foot, six-man crew factory-efficient seiners, the small tykes were the holdouts; the trolling boats were the last bastion of individuals wanting to pit wits against wily salmon. Trolling seemed the best way to provide money for men and a future for fish: odds between salmon and hook-and-line men were even-up.

Freshwater Bay was a popular lay-in for the trollers. With the fish pouring heavily into Blackfish Sound, looking out over the bay you could hardly view the sea through the masts. In the evening I'd row out and hear the wildest, tallest mix of fable and fact from fishermen tied together after a long day's labor, enjoying a mug-up of tea, brandy, or what have you. What a pool of individuals and unlimited resources—modern-day pioneers.

There was rank and file among the trollers according to how a man placed on the list of earnings for the past season. The "highliner" was Billy Proctor, five years running.

Billy was the man Malloff patterned himself after when first arriving in the wilderness. When Malloff spoke of Billy, his voice slowed and filled with a respect he never quite granted anyone else. It wasn't the big money Proctor earned—it was the wealth of values in the man himself. Malloff told me how Billy grew up, spending his first twenty-one years right here at Freshwater Bay back when it was a fish camp buying from sailing gill-netters. He told how Billy has never tasted alcohol—for his father drowned on the way home after drinking in Alert Bay—and as a young boy Billy had to do a man's work to keep the camp for his mother. The forty-six-year-old man had been to a city only once, and that was to have his boat built: the *Twilight Rock,* named after the sea mound back of Swanson that is a magnet for fish. Malloff told how Proctor has never driven a car and doesn't care to pilot anything over concrete. And his Indian arrowhead and artifact collection—over a hundred pieces, some a thousand years old—he gathers from beaches he rows into to stretch his sea legs while looking, always looking, and now museums are after all that antiquity he has gathered. Though he earns up to $100,000 in four months of fishing, he doesn't laze away the rest of the year. He works a hand-logging claim and traps fur in the winter. Once, when Malloff was hauling in wire mesh and metal poles for a proper garden fence, Billy said, "Save you all that trouble, comrade. I'll bring you some cougar piss. Sprinkle it around the border—deer won't show within a mile."

One morning, instead of a herd of diesels firing up at four A.M., only one troller headed out, cutting a thin path through my sleep. I opened my eyes but couldn't see a thing. The fog had rolled in thick. When I rowed out into the bay, I saw ghost ships turning slowly in the tide. The fog pushed the horizon in and lowered the ceiling to eye level. The fishermen's beards were covered with brilliant water beads and their tanned skins glistened.

"Naw, I ain't goin' out there to feed my boat to the rocks," said one.

"Okay, then," another replied.

"Who went out?" I asked.

"Only one boat can fish through this soup: *Twilight Rock*. Proctor knows this shoreline like the crack of his wife's ———."

"Bill Proctor has forgotten more about salmon fishing than we'll ever know," added another man.

"But how can he see out there?" I asked.

"Don't need to. He can find his way by scoping the bottom—ain't no fog underwater. He knows by the shapes down there how the shore runs."

"More shut-eye for me," one man concluded.

"Yep, no sense rippin' gear."

At noon, Proctor poked back into the bay with his hatch three-quarters full of fish, and it was only the first day of a five-day opening.

I rowed out later with a head of garden lettuce and a loaf of whole wheat bread fresh from the oven. Appreciating the home-grown and homemade grub, Billy and his deckhand invited me to stay aboard for dinner.

"No, thanks, I've already eaten—it's for you guys."

"How 'bout riding along tomorrow?" Proctor said.

"Only if you put me to work!"

"You're on."

I couldn't sleep that night for fear I'd sleep through the four A.M. alarm. I hit the deck at three forty-five expecting to wait—but Billy had already finished breakfast. He called me in for coffee. The young deckhand stumbled up the stairwell and went out on deck. Billy and I listened to tinkling in the sea.

"You know, Coast Guard told me that six out of ten stiffs they fish out of the salt-chuck have their flies down. Sport fishermen, mainly: drinking one more beer, and then when they lean over to piss clear of the side, in they go and the boat pulls away—set to troll. Imagine that— seein' your boat going away from you, radio playing, and there you startin' to freeze to death in forty-two-degree water!"

The fog had thinned to a few wisps, veils of it settling on the face cool and fresh as Billy wheeled the boat out into the Sound while Gary, the deckhand, lowered the trolling poles and fed out the gear.

A trolling boat carries two slender wooden poles fifty feet long, projecting horizontally from each side to spread four stainless steel lines. Two lines stream down from the tips of the poles (one on each side) and lines from the midpoints of the poles trail astern to float-markers thirty yards or so behind the boat. Each line is held straight down by a heavy ball of lead. Power wheels called gurdies, controlled by a foot-pedal clutch from a shaft off the main engine, bring in the lines when a fish is hooked. The actual fishing gear, the leaders and lures, are attached to the lines at intervals and trail in the water. A boat with four lines fishes forty to sixty individual pieces of gear. The idea is to mimic a school of small fish. Bells on the poles signal when a salmon hits a lure.

Covering a wall inside the *Twilight Rock* cabin was a jungle of hooks, leaders, hootchies, and flashers. Hootchies are small rubber squid stained in all shades of the rainbow. The flashers are long, rectangular chrome plates bent at odd angles, one tied to a swivel between each fishing line and steel leader, with the hootchie at the very end covering the hook. The flasher turns and wobbles through the water, reflecting light and snapping the "grass skirt" of the hootchie open in an irregular rhythm. With sixty such sets going at a similar beat, they are a sure bet to attract salmon's attention.

Billy explained that when salmon come upon a real school of herring or squid, at first they don't bite. They slam high-speed through the pack, punching with their heads and slapping their tails, then darting back to chomp the stunned ones. So the idea is to have your lures already imitating the wounded, the flasher wobble and hootchie pop triggering bites.

"But so many hootchie colors—how do you know which ones to use?" I asked.

"Depends on the color of the water, time of day, what the tide is stirring up. Salmon are finicky—always changing about what and when to eat. Have to know the ocean— slightest change makes all the difference."

As I pondered Proctor's words and looked over the palette of colors, the various lines, it was clear that trolling for salmon is both art and science.

Billy headed his forty-four-foot boat along the Swanson shoreline, running the lures close to the beaches, riding the tide just right through pocket coves. I watched in amazement as he entered hollows and bights where I didn't dare take the dory.

"Big kings like to lay in behind the rock piles in the shallows. Trick is to tease the gear over the rocks without snaggin'. A diver could make a bundle bringing up all the flashers and cannonball lead on this reef."

He swung the wheel hard over, entering a back eddy. We were carried directly toward a tall cliff. With the tip of the outrigger pole nearly tapping rock, he turned away, sweeping lures over the underwater slope. Bells jingled and both poles bounced.

Billy ran from the wheelhouse and he and Gary worked the gurdies. As salmon came up fighting, the men quick-clubbed them, then swung them off the hooks onto the enclosed deck. I wanted to jump in and help, but I couldn't find an opening. They had a dual system down pat.

There was a small wheel to steer the boat from the stern. As Billy kept hauling in fish, he asked me to steer out a ways—open water would do.

When the run was over, eighteen springs or tyees, as king salmon are called in Canada, lay on deck, most at twenty pounds, together worth well over a thousand dollars. Spring salmon fetched top dollar, for the meat is the tastiest of all salmon (flavored with fat). It was the old trade-off: you could go after, say, a load of coho, easier to catch but not weighing or worth half as much as big springs; but the springs are harder to find. King salmon fishing was Proctor's specialty. That's why he loaded up quicker and made more money than the others.

As I steered, Gary and Billy dressed the fish with flashing knives and then placed them down in the hold, on ice. We then went for three hours, up and down, back and forth along the island without a single bite. Twice Billy brought out new shades of hootchies and ran them down the poles.

As the big inboard diesel droned on, time weighed heavy without the sound of bells. To ease the monotony, Billy broke out some fish stories. He told about one year when the fishing got mighty interesting. "Two gals showed up in the thick of the fleet on their own troller and they loaded up faster than any of us—only they didn't wet a line—didn't need to. They set up shop. Traded a fuck for fish. Depending on what all extras you wanted determined how many salmon you poured into their hold. Name of the boat was *La Belle,* and if any man could shake the bells out on the tips of the poles, next time they'd give you a free go. No one ever did. One big mule was pourin' it on like steel in a smelter, but no ring-a-ding. He got suspicious and climbed out on the pole—no dinger in the bell!

"They made a ton of money before the wives got wind of it. One day, during the sockeye run, they all chartered a float plane and flew down on the party. It was some ambush!"

Just then the right-hand bell started pealing and the pole danced up and down.

"A real shaker—got a big one on!" Gary called.

Billy worked the gurdy carefully, watching the vibrations in the pole to gauge just how much fight was left in the fish. If he horsed it in too fast, he could rip the hook out if the tyee ran in the opposite direction, or if the set was weak to begin with.

Gary then bent over the side, stabbed with the gaff, and gave a two-fisted heave. A huge salmon hit the deck, slapping like the crack of a whip. Gary clubbed it over the head. Its mouth opened and closed in yawning gasps; then a shadow passed over it, the silver scales fading to gray.

I had never seen a salmon that big before. Even dead, it contained a magnificent power, muscular-thick to the last inch of head and tail. And to think that a forty-pound salmon came out of just twenty feet of water, and so close to home.

Billy turned up the volume on the "Mickey Mouse" C.B. radio that squawked and spattered across all channels with salmon talk. It blasted away day and night with men trading fishing conditions with friends and partners in secret, comic codes: "Hi yo, Silver! The Lone Ranger got Black Bart up against the wall at Cat's Ass Pass." Whoever was fishless, and cracked the code, stampeded over to cut in on the "Lone Ranger's" action.

Proctor had his followers, but even if they trailed directly behind him, he would pull fish right in front of their noses, leaving them empty-handed. There was a rumor going around that the *Twilight Rock* was rigged against the law: instead of sending a negative ground into the water, Proctor's wire was said to be live, attracting fish with a positive charge. But the real difference was that Billy didn't see the salmon merely as money in the bank. He was genuinely interested in the fish themselves, and was fascinated by the sea. He kept an invaluable logbook, describing in detail each day's fishing: computing all factors, recording variables until predictable patterns emerged. Proctor's feeling for fishing bordered on passion. More than once, after returning home after a long haul, Billy kissed his wife hello, then good-bye as he hopped into his speedboat to go sport fishing.

As we coasted into Freshwater Bay, Billy handed me a

fish "for the day's wage." I told him I had "spring" fever—couldn't wait to try for a big one on my own.

"Well, now you know where to go—but troll out deeper, too. The point off Flower Island is good."

He then said the most exciting way to catch salmon is to "do what I did when I lived here—go after 'em with a handline." He ducked into the cabin and brought out a couple "killer" hootchies, handed over a small cannonball, and told me to buy a handline with linen in it that wouldn't slice the fingers, then get a cedar stick, notch a V in the top end, and snap on a clothespin between a big knot in the line and the stick jammed into the dory gunwale. Then I'd be all set with a miniature outrigger.

With materials pared down to pure simplicity, I headed out early in the morning, tagging along behind the trolling fleet—a small mouse following the big cats. Day after long summer day I rode the carousel, catching on, snagging salmon. One morning, when our paths crossed, I lifted up to Proctor one to be proud of. He gave a blast on the horn—official notice that I was one of the bunch.

Billy was right—there was nothing to beat handline trolling, for there's nothing between you and the thrill itself. When the clothespin snapped and the knot jumped the gap, I would grab the line, dip my hands into water to cool outgoing friction, then lift, fighting line back in, hand over fist. When I was able to plop the cannonball aboard and search down through clear blue to silver flashes of salmon, I was greeted by a sight embedded in the psyche, and was forever addicted to that feeling of the sudden chomp against the fingers—your dangling question and an answer from the deep tugging on the line, hooking you. Catch a million fish, yet it's new each time—you never know what or how big until it rises slow-fight to the surface or takes air with a bursting leap.

The good trollers, the highliners, are gamblers shaving points over rock piles for the thrill that rings bells, brings money.

One late afternoon, Proctor pulled into the bay looking dead tired, his blood-red eyes ringed by dark circles. He had had engine trouble at the tail end of the previous day, then had ducked into Breakfast Bay and had been up all night jury-rigging the engine, for he could tell by the look of the sea that today's fishing would bring fat kings to top off his load.

"I say every year this is going to be my last—but then when that first southeaster blows in the spring and the sea gulls start their calling—hell—I just have to be out there."

Working forty hours straight would bury any other fisherman deep in his bunk. But not Billy. He sat on the edge of the cabin with a thin pole and spinning reel, flinging a new lure out into the bay. He cast four times and brought in four different fish: a red Irish lord, a bullhead, a dogfish, and a flounder. Before releasing each one, he held it up for a short time and talked about why the bullhead sculpin is scaleless; how the Irish lord mates; how the dogfish's teeth shear gear. Billy explained that when the flounder starts out it looks like any other fish, but after a couple days begins to lean over to one side. The eye on the underside starts migrating upward and across the head so that both eyes are on top of the body. As the eye travels, the baby flounder's skull also twists and the mouth turns upward. The parts going under lose pigment. When the fish is finally flat, it's dark above, white underneath, and hugs the sea bottom white-side down. The top fluctuates colors to blend fish into background.

Salmon Fishing

As the anchored *Twilight Rock* turned slowly in the tide, backlit by a setting sun, sea breeze lifting hair at the sides of his bald head, I saw Billy Proctor as old Neptune himself—fishing rod as wand—conjuring his subjects up from the deep.

7

~~~~~~~~~~~~~~~~~

EAGLES AND ORCAS

I had searched the sky in the United States for twenty years without seeing a bald eagle. Many days on the island I saw twenty-five at a time. With vast schools of herring ruffling the sea, the eagles swooped down out of the sky to grab fish. Dropping . . . seven feet of wing . . . dropping . . . fifteen pounds of bird . . . diving, tilting, descending like parachutes under control—*stab stab*—a few flaps to gain altitude, then wings out, herring wiggling, they would ride a thermal up to fir perches where they would tear into the fish. With wings folded in and snow-white heads set between square shoulders, they emanated fierce pride and regal command.

One morning I saw two eagles soaring high above the sea. One dipped directly under the other and flipped over on its back, extending its legs. The two hooked talons; the top eagle swung over, catapulting the other straight up. The pair met again in midair. The eagles locked up and flipped over each other, turning cartwheels as they tumbled down to the sea. A few yards from the water they parted, looping out over the sea, climbing up to where they started. The aerial affection was repeated: a nuptial display.

While out fishing, I once watched a pair of eagles soaring high overhead, one a few yards above the other. The top eagle dropped something. Just as the speck was about to fall past the bottom eagle, it shot out a leg and caught the object in its talons! I stopped the boat and rubbed my eyes.

The bottom eagle rose up above the other, then released the object, the other eagle making a spectacular over-the-shoulder grab. Three more exchanges and then the catcher flung the object into the sea. It was a spruce cone.

I wondered if the game-playing indicated intelligence at work; however, the longer I studied the bald eagle the more I saw that it is guided by instinct that thunderbolts across an unfurrowed brain. Eagles can live as long as human beings. Seventy years in the wild so finely hones instincts that at times the bird appears to reason.

A Kwakiutl told me of seeing two eagles hunting in tandem. One swooped down on a mink feeding near the water's edge. The mink, with the eagle in pursuit, darted over the low-tide rocks toward its lair. Another eagle, crouched low in nearby grass, sprang out, nailing the mink in midair as it dove for home.

One afternoon, a wedge of geese was winging over Blackfish Sound when a goose on one of the outer edges began to falter and the V pulled away.

An eagle lifted off from its pine perch, climbing up above the wavering goose. High in the sky, the raptor tucked its wings, dropping like an arrow. The goose swerved; the eagle swerved, then flipped over and under the goose, striking its talons into the downy breast. The eagle then righted itself and dropped down onto an island bluff. With its pointed beak, it rapidly plucked feathers, then tore into the warm flesh.

It happened so fast that it looked preordained, as if between the two it had all been rehearsed and this was the final performance. That it was—an instinct sharpened to pure efficiency through millions of years. There was no suffering; the end came quick and clean. In signaling weakness, the goose called death down upon itself, the eagle answering the vibrations as surely as a shark would in the water.

When I climbed the rock the next day, all that remained of the goose were its bones. They stood to the sky like the ribs of a wrecked ship.

The Inside Passage is an eagle haven, with a dense concentration of nests highly conspicuous in the shoreline trees of Swanson and nearby islands. In early spring, the bald eagle pairs prepare their nests for the birth of the young. The pairs (who mate for life) use the same nests year after year, and throughout the warming days they fly in a couple hundred pounds of sticks to repair the damage inflicted by winter storms.

An average-sized nest is six feet across and eight feet deep. The largest bald eagle nest on record was found in Florida. It was nine and a half feet wide, twenty feet deep, and weighed over two tons. The mass grew so big that it toppled the tree it was in.

Once the nest structure is woven tight, the eagles gather moss for the mattress. I would watch them cruise low over the island headlands, pulling up tufts with their talons, flapping back to the nests trailing long green streamers.

Nearing the time to lay eggs, the female crouches on her nest for an hour. Then she stands and looks down at a new egg. Incubation begins and in the following days she usually lays a second egg, and sometimes a third. The egg of the bald eagle is white and without markings. It is thick and bluntly rounded at the ends and only slightly larger than a chicken egg. During the forty days of incubation, both parents take turns warming the eggs.

Since incubation begins with the first egg, the young vary in size. The first chick has already tripled in bulk by the time the second chick hatches. A Cain and Abel rivalry begins, and it is fierce. Being larger and stronger, the first chick fights off the weaker newborn for food delivered by the parents. If the younger chick doesn't hold its own, it will die of starvation or from being battered.

The first flight usually takes place when the eaglet is ten weeks old. Prior to complete lift-off, immature birds are often seen bouncing up and down on the nest as if on a trampoline. As the eaglets spring into the air, they flap their wings, strengthening muscles and feathers. Then, once they push off from the nest, they must learn how to fly. They are guided by instinct, but they must learn what they can and can't do in the wind. The maiden flights are breathtaking as the young eagles shake, wobble, and roll all over the sky.

A common mistake for beginning fliers is that they misjudge their speed when coming in for a landing. I saw one gangly aviator hit a perch branch without throttling down. Just as he was about to overshoot the branch, he decided to grab it anyway. The momentum spun him over upside down and tossed him through the tree. He waddled out of the forest with embarrassment splayed across his face.

The bald eagle matures at five years of age. Its head and tail feathers turn from brown to white; beak and eyes take on a yellow color. The northern species stands three feet tall from talons to the top of its head and weighs between twelve and fifteen pounds. The wingspan is up to seven feet.

The female is larger than the male, and she is the fighter. It is up to her to protect the chicks from marauding great horned owls. The male eagle tends to be shy, flying away when disturbed.

The heaviest load a mature eagle can carry is ten pounds. Occasionally it will misjudge a salmon's size and hook into a twelve- or fifteen-pounder. While out in the kayak, I once spotted an eagle down on the water, bobbing over low waves. As I drew closer, I saw a flashing metallic shape underneath—a large salmon hooked to talons. The eagle was gasping for breath, wings spread limply over the pierced salmon. I then burst out laughing as the eagle spun around, then was zipped from side to side by the running fish. Putting comedy aside, I reached down and flopped both eagle and big catch into the boat. The spent bird lay over on its side, unable to release the fish because its talons were sunk in up to the hilt. However, it wasn't a good set: the sharp curves, missing the spinal cord, were buried into side meat. When the salmon flopped, the eagle squawked as it was thrown about. I quieted both by clubbing the fish over the head, and then pushed victor and vanquished overboard onto the nearest beach.

Once every few summers, a giant king salmon turns up in a seine net wearing a crown of talons. What a sight it must be to see, underwater, a salmon gliding with an eagle standing on its back—a macabre flesh-and-blood totem combination. But how long before the drowned bird finally rots away or is eaten? Once the eagle sinks talons in, the only way it can retract is if it pushes against a hard surface, then pulls away.

An amazing bald eagle power is its eyesight. It can see eight times greater than man. An experiment was conducted in which a scuba diver speared a ten-inch fish and then twitched it up on the surface. A biologist, hidden in a blind, scanned the opposite shoreline with binoculars. A bald eagle perched two miles away lifted off, swooped down, and snatched the fish.

In Kwakiutl mythology, Eagle is the Seer, with eyes so powerful that it peers far into the future. The eagle is also a totem to hunters. Many an Indian has imitated the swift, silent way the raptor kills.

The Plains and Pueblo Indians used the eagle's feathers for ceremonial purposes. In every tribe there was a catcher—a man expert in snaring wild eagles with his bare hands.

The catcher dug a pit about a yard square and two yards deep near a large tree. He laid down in the opening and assistants covered him over with branches, sod, and leaves. In the center was a thin opening for the man's hand, and branches were left fairly loose in another spot so he could peer through. A dead rabbit was placed near the hand-hole, with a tame eagle as a decoy.

Spotting the feeding bird, a soaring eagle would land in the tree. After carefully scrutinizing the area, it would descend for a share of the kill. As soon as it touched down, the Indian grabbed the eagle by the legs, flipping it over onto its back. The man tied the legs together and carried the eagle into the village, where it was tethered to a rooftop. Many eagles were captured, with only a few feathers taken from each; then the birds were freed.

Down from the eagles' breasts was also taken. In preparation for footraces, braves covered their hair, shoulders, and arms with the down. As they emerged from their shelters, onlookers threw more down into the air to add speed to their favorite runner. Old men stroked the runners' legs with eagle feathers belonging to former champions.

The eagle feather was given to reward a great deed or

for bravery in battle. You could measure a man by counting the plumes he wore in his hair.

One day I was given an eagle feather—which came as a total surprise. I was drift-fishing on a sea of glass, my mind reflecting the calm. I was asleep with my eyes open, mental circuitry closed down to a glimmer of anticipation behind the door the fish would tug open. But then I was startled by a fluttering shadow on the water. I looked up.

A large feather was falling out of the sky. My hands cupped together and lifted, imitating the swiveling motion. I rose up on my toes and met it in midair.

Two fingers grasped the quill, twirling the eagle feather in front of my eyes to affirm its actual existence. I then bent my head back and looked up. Empty blue. I wondered how in all the billions of cubic inches of the day, how did I happen to be precisely where and when a feather fell from a flying eagle!

I stopped the analysis, the calculation of odds, and accepted it as sacred—from bird to man, from wing to hand. I've made sure that, like an honored flag, my totemic banner never touches the ground.

Out in Blackfish Sound is an islet I named the Airport, for the multitude of eagles that take off and land there. I found many feathers stalled in stands of grass.

One morning, I climbed a granite bluff—the island's apex at eight hundred feet. I shinned up a spruce and sat in the crook of a branch out above the sea. Islands sprawled below like scattered puzzle pieces. What I was looking for was there.

An eagle soared in widening gyres, ascending high, higher . . . then, with a shake of the wings, tucking and sliding down over the peak of air. Thundering down, the angular wedge plunged past me. He flared his wings; wind whined through splayed feathers as he shot out across the sea, screaming with power. From a valley in the waves, thermal air thrust the eagle straight up, high up, until he was a mere dot in the blue. The current ebbed. The eagle oared the air, flew under a rock of moon, then out over the curve of sea.

From the horizon, my spirit returned reluctantly.

While fishing behind the Airport, I spotted an immature eagle sitting on a rocky point close to the sea. I thought it peculiar that the eagle was perched so low. I moved in closer and then saw trouble: one wing hung down on the ground.

I beached the dory, grabbed the salmon net, and slowly approached the eagle. It hopped away, dragging its left wing. When I cornered it against a boulder, the eagle flapped its good wing, leaned back on its tail, shot out talons, opened its beak, and hissed. I gently netted the big bird and eased it into the dory.

Waves slapped the boat. I scanned the sky. Wind doggies forewarned of a storm. Rather than risk a precarious ride to Alert Bay, I returned to the island. I released Kwee Kwa (Kwakiutl for "eagle") in the strawberry patch—a long run enclosed in mesh net. Kwee Kwa stood on her injured wing, blinking her eyes. I tossed salmon guts into the run. She stepped up onto the innards, ripping them with her beak.

The wind had risen to thirty knots, discouraging a trip to the hospital. At dark, I crept into the run and carefully approached the eagle. She didn't back away. I passed my hand in front of her. No reaction. The eyes of the sun—blind in the darkness. I gently probed the injured wing. Through a gaping hole I saw two broken bones, then smaller holes, and clotted blood throughout the wing. A shotgun blast.

The storm was raging, tossing up high waves. I wanted

professional treatment for the eagle but the open dory wouldn't offer much shelter in the rolling sea.

Later that evening, a large yacht sledded into the bay and anchored. I rowed out in the dinghy and explained the situation to the captain. He said that I could take the eagle in with them first thing in the morning.

At sunup, I put Kwee Kwa into a crate, boarded the yacht, and we pounded through the storm to the hospital. The first step was to x-ray the wing. On the floor of the x-ray room, I put Kwee Kwa on her back and grasped her ankles. By pushing a tendon I was able to clamp her talons shut. The technician stretched the injured wing out full length and took a picture. All the while the eagle was still except for the wild pounding in her chest. The x ray showed a broken radius and ulna just above the elbow of the wing.

The doctor came in, scanned the x ray, and said, "If we immobilize the wing in a wrap, the bones might mesh." We wrapped her wing tight against her torso and then decided to attempt a penicillin shot. I was certain the bird would hit the ceiling. I asked a nurse to hood the eagle by holding a cloth over its eyes. The needle entered a large thigh vein, and the doctor slowly pushed the thick fluid in. Kwee Kwa didn't flinch. I put her into the crate and we hitched a ride back to the island.

For the next two days, she devoured a big salmon, dashed back and forth, and furiously flapped her good wing whenever I came near. The second night, I went into the run and put Kwee Kwa on her back, but before tightening the wrap I looked in at the wound. I was horrified. It percolated with maggots. A quarter of her wing had been eaten away.

I was eyeing my rifle when I remembered that the hospital receptionist had given me the phone number of a man "who's up on eagles." I got through to him over the radio/phone and he told me about a veterinarian in Victoria who had successfully treated gun-shot eagles.

At daybreak I put the eagle into the crate, went to Alert Bay, and at the small airport arranged for Kwee Kwa to be flown to the vet. While waiting for the plane, I heard thrashing in the crate. I opened the door. A tremor lifted her . . . she came down dead.

I paced for miles on the runway, feeling rage burn inside. On the screen behind my eyes I kept seeing the eagle soaring free, then falling from the sky, her wing shattered by a gun in the hands of a demented man.

I took a talon and the long bone from Kwee Kwa's good wing. I went out to the spot where I found her, lowered her into the sea, and watched the tide carry the eagle away.

Out of the bone I fashioned a flute.

A few days later, I paddled the baidarka out into the middle of Blackfish Sound and blew a stream of high-pitched notes through the bone. As if in response, a pod of killer whales appeared with explosions of breath and tall dorsal fins cleaving the sea.

The difference between seeing a zoo Shamu and a wild killer whale is like the difference between seeing Tarzan on display in a straightjacket and romping free through his jungle.

The first time I encountered the whales was the previous summer, just after arriving on the island. Malloff and an Indian fisherman, between belts of rum, were strumming guitars and singing every song they could recall. When I went out onto the beach for fresh air, amplified in the quiet darkness I heard what sounded like steam bursting from pipes: spouting whales—the very breath of the sea. A pod was in Freshwater Bay. They began lobtailing:

lifting their tails up above the surface and then smacking them down. *Boo-boom* echoed off the granite bluffs. They then took turns breaching—leaping out of the sea—with phosphorescent plankton, pulses of electric blue and white, streaming off them. It was a spectacular sound and light show!

My experiences with the killer whales were like climbing a ladder—only the whales arranged the rungs. Once they accepted me into their midst, I slowly got closer; by degrees, they revealed more and more of themselves to me.

The culmination came when I was out in the small dinghy rowing life into stagnant muscles. I settled into an even rhythm, watching the house shrink away and savoring the calm mental state created by physical exertion.

Suddenly a tremendous splash drowned my meditation.

I spun around on the seat and saw a killer whale—a big bull—fifty yards away at a nine o'clock position. Then a younger male spouted at ten o'clock, and a female rolled up straight off the bow. From the way she raised her head before she went under, I sensed she was coming straight for me. I pulled in the oars, waiting, my heart thumping in my ears.

The whale rose up a few feet away. I looked into a lucid blue eye. She spouted and I breathed her breath. There was a mere inch or two between her side and the edge of the skiff. My hand went out. I touched her on the back behind the towering fin. The flesh quivered. Her back wheeled under my fingertips, her skin like supple satin.

I came to back in the cabin—sitting at the round table—not remembering rowing in, so absorbed was I in the direct contact with the whale that permeated my consciousness. I touched the whale; she touched me; and what passed between us changed me forever.

Later that night I read from Ortega y Gasset: "So many things fail to interest us simply because they don't find in us enough surfaces on which to live, and what we have to do then is to increase the number of planes in our mind, so that a much larger number of themes can find a place in it at the same time."

The killer whales inspired me to expand my planes and points of intersection. After observing them, I wanted to seek out and employ all inherent powers. Occasionally my fingertips tingled with wild energy. It led me on.

The presence of the killer whales made me feel that every time I went out on Blackfish Sound I was embarking on a great adventure. Even though I fished nearly every day, it never became routine, for I was always on the look-out for the explosions of breath, towering fins, spectacular leaps. Sometimes weeks would pass without a trace of the whales, but their absence only sharpened my eagerness to see them. Then—they arrived when I least expected. I would be sitting inside at the round table sipping tea, reading. I'd lift my head to rest my eyes by looking out the window—there! A pod charging across the Sound, dorsal fins flying. The sight always pulled me to my feet. I dashed out either in the kayak or dory to join them or, if they were too far ahead, I stood at the window watching, absorbing their beauty and might.

I was trolling for salmon one morning when two killer whales came out of the water, leaping straight up. They fell onto their backs, crashing onto the surface—then disappeared underwater. I shut off the engine and followed a premonition, looking over my shoulder. They came up again a few yards off the stern. Instead of breaching, they lifted only the upper halves of their bodies out of the water and pirouetted a graceful turn, then sank down, sending a whirling ripple across the surface that encircled the boat.

I tossed my head back and shouted, releasing my solitary joy at witnessing such a colossal ballet. This island boy felt least alone surrounded by the whales, for I felt sure I was in the presence of other rational, cognizant beings.

The brain size of the killer whale (not actually a whale but the largest dolphin) is 6,000 cubic centimeters. The average human brain is 1,400 cubic centimeters. Many people explain the difference with the maxim, "The bigger the body, the bigger the brain needed to move it." However, only a small portion of the killer whale's brain—less than ours—is concerned with the output of mechanical skills. The killer whale, being without manipulative hands, has a brain larger than ours in the general association area, which in us functions as memory and conceptual thought.

While psychologist Paul Spong was pioneering the study of killer whale intelligence, he discovered that the captive Orca often trains the trainer. In his chapter "The Whale Show" from *Mind in the Waters,* Dr. Spong reported, "Early one morning I was sitting on a training platform at the edge of Skana's pool dangling my bare feet in the water. Skana approached me slowly, as she usually did, until she was a few inches from my feet. Then, suddenly, and without warning, she opened her mouth and slashed it quickly across my feet, so that I could feel her teeth dragging across the tops and soles of my feet. Naturally, though probably with a very slow reaction time, I jerked my feet out of the water. After a pause for reflection and recovery from shock, I put my feet back into the water. Again Skana approached and slashed her open mouth across my feet. Again I jerked them out of the water and after awhile put them back in, only to have her and myself repeat the procedure. We went around in this circle ten or eleven times, until finally I could sit calmly with my feet in the water, controlling the urge to flinch as she flashed her teeth across my feet. Then she stopped. Remarkably, I no longer felt afraid. She had very effectively and quickly deconditioned my fear of her."

After twelve years of examining cetacean intelligence, Dr. John Lilly, the founder of The Communication Research Institute for the biomedical study of communication between man and dolphin, concluded that "the limits are not in them, the limits are in us."

Man has had his brain for one million years. The killer whale has had its for thirty million. We only employ approximately one-hundredth of the newest part of our brain—the neocortex. Why travel through outer space when we have so much farther to go within ourselves? The neocortex should be our new frontier, challenging pioneers to explore the mysteries and magnitudes of the one-eighth-inch thick, infolded continent. It could be that the whales and dolphins have already charted the course, but to grasp that information we have to overcome a communication barrier. The cetaceans do not respond to our verbal language. They do react to our music, for it resembles their own mode of communication. The ancient Greeks first described the cetaceans' attraction to music. One myth tells how Orpheus was kidnapped and taken aboard a boat. Out at sea he played his lyre, attracting dolphins. He jumped overboard and they carried him ashore.

Numerous times when Malloff and friends were playing music, the whales moved into Freshwater Bay and lolled on the surface, as if listening attentively. However, the music had to be live—tapes and records did not have the same allure.

While watching a violin maker at work in his shop in Vancouver, I asked why the Stradivarius violins are considered the best. The elderly man raised his eyebrows, set down his tool, and then folded his hands. "I'll let you in on a secret, my boy, Antonio Stradivarius's secret." He paused to look around, adding a touch of drama before disclosing the information.

"He was walking on a beach in Italy one day when he

found a big lump of waxy substance. After examining it closely, he melted it down in his shop and applied the paraffin as a sealant to a violin he had just finished. The sounds were amplified and the tone . . . crystal clear. I looked into this ambergris, as it is called. It comes only from the sperm whale, which feeds on giant squid down deep that have hard beaks for mouths. These beaks lodge inside the whale, but the intestines, they secrete an oily wax that coats the beaks, preventing them from harming the whale's innards. When these lumps grow too cumbersome, the whale passes them out into the sea, and some, they float in to the shore. . . ."

I clapped my hands. "What a connection! Ambergris starts as an irritant—just like the pearl—and the end result is the same: a creation of beauty. How fantastic—musical whales 'filling' concert halls throughout the world!"

A musician from California came to Blackfish Sound with an underwater drum he had made. The skin was held above water, the opening submerged. He beat a congo bongo and from the sea came what sounded like Coltrane sax runs. The whales did not mimic the drum. They played along with it: a jam session between members of the group "Mammal."

The killer whales wend their way through the sea and communicate with one another by emitting a series of sonic clicks, spacing them so that the outgoing clicks either interfere or don't interfere with the incoming echoes. The clicks can be high-pitched and travel a short distance or low-pitched and travel far. Killer whales can sputter one thousand clicks per second and still interpret the sound echoes.

The echoes are received through the jaws and the hollow area in the head known as the melon. The reverberations are then synthesized by the brain, supplying the killer whale with the texture, shape, speed, direction, and density of the object. Their sonar also supplies them with a sound picture of one another.

Dr. John Sutphen wrote in *Mind in the Waters* (in his chapter "Body State Communication Among Cetaceans"): "From what is now known about resolving capabilities of the dolphin's sonar and from certain well established principles of physiologic morphology of internal organs and tissues, it is reasonable to assume that Cetaceans are aware of each other's health and general well-being. Cancers and tumors must be self-evident. Strokes and heart attacks are as obvious as moles on our skin. . . . They would be constantly aware of a considerable portion of each other's emotional state. The psychophysiological alterations of sexual arousal, fear, depression and excitement may be impossible to hide . . ."

One of Jacques Cousteau's earliest experiences with dolphins occurred when he was in a boat over an Indian Ocean reef and looked down into the clear water. He saw fifteen dolphins poised on their tails, sitting on the bottom in a group, clicking and whistling as if holding a conference.

In *The Cosmic Connection* Carl Sagan wrote, "Is it possible that the intelligence of cetaceans is channeled into the equivalence of epic poetry, history, and elaborate codes of social interaction? Are whales and dolphins like human Homers before the invention of writing, telling of great deeds in years gone by, in the far reaches of the sea? . . ."

Many people concede that cetaceans are intelligent, but I often hear, "Surely what elevates us above them is our culture, our art." But for most people art is an escape— an inspiring stimulus that helps them to endure the onslaught of everyday reality. The ultimate life is when the art and the life are one. Could it be that cetaceans "sing" when they speak, "paint" when they breach, "dance" when they swim? Could it be that they have no art because they do all things beautifully?

The cetaceans have an intelligence that may surpass our own. Being nonmanipulators, they relate umbilically to their environment.

Sixty million years ago, the whale's ancestors lived on land. In the present-day killer whale's flippers are the bones of five fingers, a wrist, an arm. The bones situated near the anal region are remnants of a pelvis and two legs. Hind legs are present in the fetus until the eighth month. The two nostrils in the blowhole migrated from the front of the face to the top of the head.

Perhaps the "dawn" whales entered the sea because food was more abundant and easier to capture in the liquid depths. Perhaps they welcomed the buoyancy, being able to maneuver their ponderous bulk as if weightless.

The killer whale's range is global. They are found in all seven seas and in many rivers. They are usually sighted within two hundred miles of the continental shelf, where their prey is most plentiful. They are territorial, with individual pods ruling vast stretches of sea. During the winter, some of the British Columbia pods migrate to California waters. Other groups stay here year-round.

Each pod consists of a senior bull with a harem of cows and their young. The adult male is twenty-five feet long and can weigh up to ten tons. His dorsal fin stands a towering six feet. A mature female is twenty feet long, weighs eight tons, and her curved fin is three to four feet tall.

Individual whales are discerned by the shape of their dorsal fins. Besides each differing slightly in profile, many fins have telltale scars, notches, and broken cartilage from encounters with logs, rock piles, propellors. On the back, just behind the fin, is a grey saddle patch. As with human fingerprints, no two saddle patches are alike.

The male and female mate on the surface in a horizontal position. They intertwine flippers; the male inserts the tip of a four-foot penis into the female's vaginal slit. Their grunts and cries can be heard for miles.

The gestation period is sixteen months. The baby is born underwater—tail first so that it doesn't drown. As the baby emerges from the birth canal, the umbilical cord snaps spontaneously, then immediately the mother or another female of the pod pushes the baby up to the surface for its first breath. A newborn infant is seven feet long and weighs four hundred pounds.

The mother's milk, high in fat content, resembles cottage cheese; the baby whale rapidly puts on weight, for it needs a suit of blubber to insulate itself in the forty-two-degree water.

Killer whales can dive thousands of feet and stay submerged for thirty minutes on one breath. When they sound, they roll their tail flukes up out of the water, descending vertically. If they are traveling on the surface, they spout every twenty to thirty seconds and can swim in bursts of thirty miles an hour.

Killer whales suffer from the same illnesses that plague humans. People working with captive whales have given them the flu and vice versa. The whales develop ulcers, and the older ones have hardening of the arteries and heart attacks brought on by their high-cholesterol diet. Under a microscope, a diseased tissue sample from a killer whale looks identical to a human's.

Like human yogis, the whales know how to do circular breathing and can control their heartbeat and blood pressure. Captive killer whales that are repeatedly jabbed in the tail for a blood sample simply shut off the blood supply to the sore spot and have to be pricked elsewhere. When the wild whale sounds, it conserves oxygen by shutting off blood to parts of the body not needed during the dive.

Killer whales' breathing, unlike man's, is conscious. When a whale surfaces, it must gauge wave size before inhaling, and young whales have drowned in severe storms. When a pod is resting together on the surface, they synchronize their breathing.

Today the killer whale is commonly referred to as Orca, from its Latin classification *Orcinus Orca*. Many cetologists feel that Orca is a less threatening name. However, Orca is indeed a killer: he relentlessly hunts all marine mammals and fish for food.

British Columbia fishermen reported seeing hundreds of salmon leap out of the water, piling up on the rocks to elude their attackers. One fisherman saw a dolphin leap high above the surface; at the peak of the leap, a killer whale surged up and caught the dolphin in its jaws.

With their powerful tails killer whales often slap sea lions high into the air before devouring them—like a cat toying with its mouse, only in this case the "mouse" weighs close to a ton!

A Kwakiutl informed me that "a killer whale can swallow a seal as easily as a person downs an oyster." They have forty-four conical teeth lining both jaws, but the teeth are used to grasp prey rather than chew it. Instead of "Jaws" it's more like "Gulp." Everything is swallowed whole, or in large chunks.

The Kwakiutls call the killer whales "sea wolves" for the manner in which they hunt in cooperative packs. The wolves of the deep possess a natural camouflage. Their black and white skin patterns merge into the wavering underwater shadows.

The killers attack the largest creature on earth, the blue whale, only for its tongue. A phalanx forces open the giant mouth and the second wave rushes in to rip out the delicacy. The sea wolves lurk outside the Baja lagoons, the breeding grounds and nurseries of the gray whales. As the grays leave the sheltered lagoons to enter open ocean for the long migration north, the killers try to ambush unwary calves.

Being at the top of the ocean's food chain, the killer whale does not know fear—unless man has introduced it. Sixty percent of all killer whales caught and examined by scientists have had bullet holes in their bodies.

Killer whales and scuba divers peacefully share the same habitat in Blackfish Sound. The whales glide by, sonar clicking, eyes shifting as they examine the underwater visitors. They seem to recognize and respect the human intelligence, perhaps knowing full well that it is a two-edged sword.

Dr. Paul Spong reports in *Mind in the Waters*: "I know of just two instances in which orcas have actually attacked and killed people. Perhaps the most interesting thing about these cases is that in each of them the attack, if not the result, was justified. I will relate one of these stories by way of introduction to *Orcinus orca*."

"In 1956 two loggers working on a hillside in British Columbia were skidding logs down the slope into the water. Noticing a pod, or family group, of orcas passing below, one of the loggers deliberately let go a log which skidded down and hit one of the whales in the back, apparently injuring but not killing it. The whales went away. That night, as the loggers were rowing back to camp, the whales reappeared and tipped the boat over. One man vanished, the one who had let the log go. The other man was not touched and survived to tell the tale."

Long ago, a Kwakiutl boy spent many hours preparing himself for a Moment of Truth. He sprinted barefoot over long, slippery logs. He fasted and meditated, toughening and expanding his inner self. When he felt ready, the youth got into a canoe with two paddlers. They approached a killer whale sleeping on the surface. The paddlers were careful not to lift their oars out of the sea, lest the dripping water awaken the whale. They swung up alongside the tail; the boy jumped out onto the whale, dashing over the back to the top of the head, then soaring back into the waiting canoe. Returning to the village, the boy was honored as a *skookum*, or powerful man.

Loren Eiseley and others have written about "cosmic loneliness"—the state man will be reduced to if he continues his rapid slaughter of other species. Human beings fail to realize that in destroying other forms of life, we shrink our own range of possibilities.

On the slate-gray cliff of a nearby island, six feet above the sea, an old Kwakiutl painted something, perhaps a self-portrait. It is a person's face: an oval with round eyes. It is the face of a killer whale: elevated forehead and pointed teeth. Looking at it over and over, I could not separate man from whale: two made one; each was the other.

8

NORTHERN AUTUMN

The waning sun tracked a southerly path. Trees flamed and the leaves sailed down, scuttling over the hardening earth. The north wind nipped at all creatures.

Autumn in the North is but a brief prelude to the winter fugue. It goads summer spendthrifts into becoming industrious hoarders. Along with the squirrels, Malloff, Beth, and I prepared for the barren months. We smoked salmon, canned fruits and vegetables, hunted geese, ducks, deer. Out in the Sound we lassoed drifting logs, towed them home, and bucked them up into firewood.

Indian summer arrived, but we were not seduced. We continued stockpiling, knowing that the warm days passed as quickly as the falling leaves. My muscles sprouted as I swung Malloff's twelve-pound maul through knotty pine. As I smashed the rounds open, I sang a Thoreau saying: "When you—CHOP—firewood, you warm—TWICE."

In the evening, feeling clean and relaxed after a hot

bath, I walked over the battleground, pressing wood chips down into the earth. As I surveyed the growing woodpile, I sniffed the leather scent of fir, the pungent spice of cedar. Air came in off the water fresh and cold. To stay warm, I drew into myself, my mind now "all-muscle"—singing the body electric. Bursting with a new surge of energy, I shadowboxed in the moonlight.

Few boats came into the bay now. The fair-weather adventurers had returned to the distant cities. Every day, Malloff and I worked side by side for long hours, milling lumber or clearing trails—pausing to munch an apple, chug a beer—then back into the harness of hard, physical work.

One bright afternoon, I put the long-handled scythe into the dory and went out alone to the headland on Flower Island. I climbed up to the flat of tall grass and swung the blade in time with the slapping sea.

I paused to look out over vast blue sea rippling against mountain walls. It was pure wilderness before my eyes: not an inkling of man. Surrounded by such immensity, I wondered if I was even there. I looked down at my feet and lifted my hands, to affirm my existence.

As the blade whisked through the grass, I thought of the Russian peasants and how Will Malloff continued their ways. I thought of Tolstoy's search for the ideal peasant, and how he found them in the Dukhobors, of whom Malloff was a descendant. The long, wooden handle felt alive in my hands, as if from the worn grain I picked up vibrations from hands long ago. I felt their calluses hard as coins.

And a working tool so pleasing to the eyes. The sweeping line of the steel blade was a curve of beauty—the lofty samurai sword brought down to earth, put to work. Many of Malloff's hand tools were objets d'art. Antique collectors made offers, but no deal. "Tools are meant to be used, not hung on walls," Malloff announced. "No accident that these old tools work best. They do minimum damage to the earth and keep you strong in the process."

The scythe literally got me into the swing of things. The tool and I worked together. The motion originated at a point back of my knees, then curved around my waist and up through the long handle of my arms into the scythe, which transformed and then returned the energy. My form of motion was shaped by the form of the scythe. Back and forth we swung, a dance of duplicates. And no noise or stink from a brand-new "Weed Eater." There was the slap of the sea, the hiss of steel through grass, and a smile on the face of a worker.

I raked the fallen grass with the tip of the scythe and carried the sheaves down the slope to pile them in the dory. Back home, I laid out a ladder horizontally—elevated with a stump under each end—and spread the long grass out across the rungs. A week later, I stowed the dry straw under the house: winter bedding for the dogs and pigs.

Saturday afternoons, CBC Radio broadcast the opera live from the Met. I turned the volume up full-blast so I could hear *La Bohème, Boris Godunov,* and *Madama Butterfly* while working outside. Man's finest sound filled the wilderness. The tones crescendoed off the granite bluffs and soared out over the sea. Pavarotti's voice was enough to make singing whales envious!

Autumn on the island was my favorite season. The summer heat and procession of people had vanished, and now the air was knife-edge keen. There was great reach and clarity in the sky. The blue was so transparent that the planets were still visible at midmorning. The north wind infused me with endless energy. I worked with arms and back all day, and then, fully charged, wrote and read into the night. I'd snatch a couple hours sleep, then burst out of bed at sunrise to have at it all over again.

I frequently looked up from my work to follow wedges of geese winging south. Hour after hour, day after day, more and more rushed over the island. At night, on the surface of sleep, I heard the droves yodeling from peaks of air as they followed the points of stars.

One morning a flock of snow geese dropped down into the bay. After splashing in, they all sat still. The spent fliers had lifted off from the Arctic only a few days before, their white plumage heralding the snow that would soon fall from the wind they rode. Now and then, here and there, one goose flicked a webbed foot and glided aimlessly among the others. The tight flock reminded me of a group of gypsies I had seen in the back hills of Spain. Both groups emanated the same all-for-oneness, a primitive otherworldliness, and the wisdom that comes from wandering.

When the sun moved four hours from where it was when they landed, the snow geese began to stir. They beaked feathers into proper positions, stretched and shook their necks. They then bunched together like runners before a marathon. A big goose paddled out of the pack and lifted up on its tail as it revved its wings. The leader took off, with the pack following—necks extended like lances, wings threshing the air. As they climbed up into the wide expanse, each goose assumed a position in the serried chevron. The leader cleaved the air in front; the others fanned out into the sides of the V, flying wingtip to wingtip, each downbeat creating an updraft under the wing of the adjacent bird. They rode their wave of air over Blacknee Pass; then the swaying formation corrected south down Johnstone Strait.

A divorced woman once said to me, "I envy the geese. They mate for life and get to travel." From a Kwakiutl I learned that if one of the pair dies, the bachelor or widow then becomes a scout. The scouts are the first to descend down into a bay. If hunters open fire, the rest of the flock has time to veer away.

Squadrons of ducks, while traveling south along the Inside Passage flyway, dipped down into our front yard—Freshwater Bay. Word was out among the feathered congregation that even though man was in sight, the water was a safe sanctuary.

Early mornings, I peered through mist rising off the water . . . there! . . . and there!—the vibrant announcements of wood ducks, mergansers, mallards, and harlequins. How freshly painted the colors looked as they emerged out of the fog: the wood duck's contrasts of primary tones, the harlequin's multicolored patches, the mallard's scintillating head that seemed more a sound than a color. But how drab the females looked next to the flashy drakes. Much like their human counterparts, I thought: the males do all the showing off, while the females stand by holding the world together.

The last wisps of mist burned away, revealing the bay as an airport busy with arrivals and departures. Incoming flocks found parking space off the side in a calm bight. Mainstay groups gabble-gossiped as the new arrivals quietly hunkered down into themselves, recuperating from the arduous miles of flight. When not snoozing, the ducks preened to maintain their waterproof plumage. Their beaks spread oil over the feathers from a gland at the base of the tail. The raking motion also zips up the interlocking structure of feather barbs. Each main shaft or quill sprouts about six hundred hooks on each side to form the familiar vane of the feather. Each of the twelve hundred barbs puts out four hundred smaller barbs called barbules, each of which again produces a score or two of tinier hooks known as barbicels. The complete interwoven mesh of one major feather contains some thirty million barbicels, and the entire duck is encased in several billion of the tiny interlocking hooks. No wonder water runs off a duck's back. Once it hits the feathered chain mail, it has no other choice but to dribble away.

When spooked by a roaming mink or the speeding dory, the ducks took off in bunches, wing-sprinting low over the water, veering tight turns in unison, then splashing down exactly where they were before they fled. The "old squaws" took forever to get airborne. Webbed feet smacked the surface as the roly-polies struggled to lift off.

Suddenly, one morning, there were no ducks in the bay. Diminishing daylight tripped the switch that sent them on their way south. The bay seemed empty and drab without the living colors. The cormorants were the only birds around. Compared to the compact ducks, they looked like gangsters with their gangly forms outfitted in slick, coal-black, bedraggled feathers. A pack of cormorants standing helter-skelter on a rock pile with wings half crooked look as if they could take their place in Edgar Allen Poe's pantheon of ominous creatures. *Cormorant* is a corruption of *corvus marinus*, which is Latin for "sea crow." Cormorants are visible nearly all of the day because they're extremely efficient hunters, capturing their fill of food in half an hour.

Cormorants may look ill at ease hauled up on the rocks, but underwater they are agile and fast, diving down to two hundred feet, wings beating, feet running as they pursue herring and small cod. Their permeable feathers reduce buoyancy and allow the hunters to drop smoothly through the sea, giving fish scant warning of their approach.

In China, the cormorant has been trained by man to do the fishing. A ring is fitted around its neck and then the bird is lowered over the side of the boat. Following instinct, it dives, catches a fish in its beak, and returns to the surface. The attendant then grabs the fish away. During the workday, the cormorants are fed to keep them fueled, but not enough to satisfy their hunger.

Late September mornings, I went off with bowl in hand to collect blackberries. I popped them, dew-wet and sun-warm, rapid-fire into my mouth and squashed them on my tongue, savoring the exquisite bursts of sweetness. A favorite breakfast was blackberry pancakes—if there were any berries left in the bowl by the time I got home.

Around the berry thickets were bear tracks and manure mounds resembling red jam. I was startled to see that we shared the small island with a black bear. When I told Malloff about seeing signs of the bear, he wasn't surprised. He explained that he never hunted the bear, for then he would have to "train" a new one all over again. Years ago, when the youngster had come down to investigate the clearing, the Ridgeback dogs had run him off with bites in the butt.

"If I shoot this one, who knows what the next bear will be like? A new one would move in to claim the island and he might be very persistent about tasting all the exotic meat around here!" Malloff explained.

One October full moon night, I went out in the baidarka. No destination. I paddled just enough to keep warm, zigzagging across the Sound, looking for whatever the swollen moon might reveal.

The flat sea reflected a gossamer sheen. There was so much light I had to remind myself it was night. The kayak seemed to lift away, floating through soft, silvery space.

I then spotted something interrupting the luminescence, redefining water. It was a large head that, at first, I thought to be a sea lion's, but then rather than curvet, the animal smashed its way through the sea. I heard *Hoo-whoosh hoo-whoosh*. It sounded like a steam locomotive. It was a bear.

I swung out of its way, not wanting the tired bruin to

mistake the baidarka for a log. The bear chugged past, its wake lifting the bow and rolling under my hips. I trailed behind about twenty yards, traveling the flat water in the center of the V. The bear kept on a direct path for an island. It spat and snorted, the big behemoth struggling to keep its sensitive nose high and dry.

Nearing the island, the bear oared with thick arms as its feet searched out the bottom. It dipped down, then sprang forward, tearing through sheets of water, loping up onto the beach. There on crushed-clamshell white, the black bear stopped and shook a mist that rose up into a moonbow of silver and blue. The colors flared, then dissolved as the bear stepped out of the nimbus and trundled into the woods.

Bear, wolf, deer, even cougar swam island to island in search of food. They usually traveled under a full moon, in the flow of the tide.

After shadowing the bear, I dreamed nightly of wolf packs running their legs through the sea; a cougar, whiskers aloft, churning past a kicking buck with rack swaying like a rocking chair; a killer whale approaching a lumbering bear, the lords of land and sea swimming side by side, measuring the output of the other's power.

The island produced fantastic dreams, rich with exotic flora and human–animal exchanges—magical fables that unfolded so vividly that, upon awakening, I was convinced that they had actually happened. I had a difficult time calling them dreams. I identified with the African tribe that knows nocturnal visions as reality and the day's activities as illusionary dream time.

Life on the island was often that way. Night fed day. Closed-eye happenings opened up fresh territory to fulfill when awake. Instead of daily experiences being digested later that night by the subconscious, it was as if the subconscious originated experiences, which later materialized in moments of déjà vu.

One night in my sleep, I saw myself in the dory heading out to investigate high-pitched cries coming from the next bay over. As I rounded the point, I saw a baby killer whale stranded high on the beach. It hadn't been there long, for it was writhing back and forth, but its frantic efforts only dug it deeper into the sand. The bay was crowded with killer whales spy-hopping. The mother whale was dashing back and forth across the retreating tide trying to reach her baby, on the verge of beaching herself. As I waited for the tide to turn, I cut kelp streamers and pulled them into the dory. I then weaved around the rising columns of whales to the beach and calmed the baby by humming a lullaby as I tied a line around the base of its tail and padded the rope by wrapping it in the kelp fronds. As the tide lapped under the infant, I slowly increased the engine speed: the line drew taut, and the whale slid into the bay. The other whales zoomed around her, filling the air with a storm of sonic relief. The baby lifted her tail so I could untie the rope, and after seeing the whale swimming on an even keel, I started for home. Suddenly the dory lifted—two whales surfaced under the boat, heaving it up, stopping me in midair. The other whales dove deep out of sight . . . then the surface boiled with hundreds of red snapper—all intact, alive, yet stunned. The whales slapped the fish up into the boat with their flippers—but they loaded the dory so full, so fast, that it started to sink. Then, with one unified flip of their tails, the whales created a great wave that heaved the heavy boat ashore. I woke up when the dory pounded the beach.

Months later—late in winter—I was hollow with hunger. I had run out of supplies and there was no sign of Malloff returning with groceries. The sea was too hostile to go the twelve miles to Alert Bay for grub. But I couldn't stomach another limpet and had had my fill of sea lettuce. I craved fresh fish, but the salmon were long gone upriver, and when I tried all the cod holes, not a single bite.

Motoring back toward Freshwater Bay, I stared down into the dory, the empty chasm looking exactly how my stomach felt.

As I came alongside "Whale Bay," for a quick instant my mind replayed the dream. When I focused ahead, I expected to see something and did. Two bright orange objects were floating on the surface. At first they looked like boat bumpers gone astray, but then the rubber floats focused into red snappers. I cut the engine. As the dory stopped by the fish, to make sure, I looked around. It felt, it was the same place where the whales had served up their thanks in my dream.

I leaned over the side and touched one of the snappers. I should have been shocked but I wasn't. The dream had been real, so why not the fish? Not as many, and not a killer whale in sight, but here was the food I needed.

Swollen air bladders protruded from gaping mouths and eyes had popped to their outer limits. Losing their grip on the deep, the fish had exploded to the surface. I remembered a Kwakiutl fisherman saying that if killer whales are hunting down across the ocean floor, in fright the big cod sometimes race away too high. The sudden lack of sea pressure sends a bottom fish to the ceiling like a helium balloon cut from its string.

The snappers were recent arrivals, for their gills were slamming open and shut. When I grabbed the ten-pounders up by their tails, protesting muscles shook my hands. Not a scale missing from their gaudy skins, and my poking finger felt meat firm and fresh. I thanked the whales, and the fish for offering themselves up.

Twisting the throttle grip wide open, I thought of Carl Jung's saying: "Proceed from the dream outward." Indeed!

The Inside Passage is real dream country. Even on land you are moved. The tides that carry the great whales move the bulk of your thoughts just as effortlessly. On the islands, the surrounding sea enters your subconscious, creating a rippling mirror that reflects reality from many perspectives. There is no concrete or asphalt to fix attitudes, harden dreams. The world around constantly flows in many levels, swirling deep fathoms into you, loosening holdfasts and safeguards, stirring up sediment, provoking protean change.

I now understood why, to the Kwakiutls, life often assumed the reality of myth.

9

KWAKIUTL INDIANS

Many of the adventures I was having in remote wilderness originated thousands of miles away, in the very civil Lilly Rare Book Library at Indiana University, a vaultlike building holding thousands of rare tomes that attracted scholars from all over the world. As an undergraduate, I worked there as a page, going into the stacks to retrieve whatever book a reader located in the card catalog. One day I filled a request for *The North American Indian, Being a Series of Volumes Picturing and Describing the Indians of the U.S. and Alaska* by Edward Sherrif Curtis, in twenty volumes. It took two full carts to wheel the books down into the reading room. A German professor, researching and writing a book on American Indians, lifted his hands, rubbing fingers across palms, then reached to start in on the treasure. He told me that he had searched for years trying to find a complete set of the photographs; this was one of only three in existence.

Herr Schmidt stayed for a week, last to leave every late afternoon and waiting on the steps for the doors to open in the morning. In between deliveries, I looked over his shoulder, mesmerized by the mystical images of Native Americans.

When I returned the folios, I remembered the shelf and spent all of my lunch hours roaming the West, looking in on Geronimo and Cochise, chasing buffalo instead of eating peanut butter and jelly sandwiches. As I progressed through the volumes, my favorite pictures were those of the northern Indians: the Eskimos, and especially the dramatic Kwakiutls, to which Curtis had devoted the largest folio. I also discovered the journals of Captain Cook, the first European to explore the Northwest coast, and devoured an ethnography of the Kwakiutls written by cultural anthropologist Franz Boas at the turn of the century.

During my lunch hours in the library, I was swept back through time, seeing cedar longhouses lined together on a narrow beach between tall forest, flat sea, a totem pole in front of each house displaying the lineage of the families within. The chief, squat and powerful, entered the largest house—walking up the bottom of the Raven's open beak that clapped shut behind him. Out at sea, twenty men, in a canoe carved from a mighty cedar tree, paddled with only the strength of a song as they brought a whale home—the beast that had towed them three suns out to sea. I read of how the Kwakiutls were the most artistic of all the Indian tribes, for the sea so abundantly provided them with food that they could spend the long winter months devoted to storytelling, art, and theater— all of which culminated in the Potlatch, "The Giving." The villagers carried into the feast house an outpouring of smoked salmon, seal, whale meat, along with art treasures such as lavish bowls, wooden chests made from a single cedar plank steamed around, mounds of woven blankets, rattles, masks—all carved with stylistic totemic motifs, the very forms creating function. A huge feast bowl would be in the shape of a killer whale, filled with eulachon fish oil, with the top handle as the dorsal fin. The guests, a neighboring tribe, arrived in eight to ten canoes with thirty people in each, moving together straight in across the bay, the paddlers creating rhythm for each clan dancer dressed as a howling wolf, flapping eagle, or big bear climbing the high canoe prow—making a grand entrance in the eyes of the host chief and his people, who sang a song of welcome. The hosts led their guests through the next four days, unfurling years of preparations. Seating positions and gifts were given out according to rank, while orators boasted of the host chief's many accomplishments. Interspersed among the recitations were eating contests as canoes full of food were set out between the tribes. As rain and wind lashed the outer world, the shake of rattles, guttural songs brought out the supernatural ancestor-beings in the forms of dancers wearing elaborate costumes and masks with eyes that opened and closed, beaks that sprang apart to reveal the human face inside. In the flickering shadows shamans worked sleight of hand and threw their voices around the big hall through hidden kelp tubes. There was the frenzied entrance of the *Hamatsa*—the entire physical reenactment of man's evolution from wild cannibal to social being of rank and order. Dancing, speeches, theatrical productions, food kept coming hour after hour that satiated all the senses. The chief buried his guests under gifts, depleting the wealth of his village. He took his coppers—plaques of beaten raw copper, a monetary unit worth four thousand blankets—tossing them into the fire, ordering his best canoe chopped into four pieces and added to the blaze. He pulled a rope, opening the mouth of the Vomiter, a carved effigy on the ceiling, spewing down a stream of valuable eulachon oil, raging the fire. While seated close, the rival chief didn't flinch, though his blanket smoldered. With flames licking the roof timbers, the host chief didn't show the slightest worry, as it was a weakness to be concerned about material matters, while the guests and fire took away all that he and his people had. The Kwakiutls accumulated wealth only for the status it awarded them when they gave it away. They weren't left destitute—it was a big loan with high interest; so as not to lose face, the guest chief had to hold his own Potlatch, try to outdo in giving what his people had received. In this way possessions were always on the move—chiefs fighting wars with property, instead of weapons. The more I read, the more I was impressed with this "primitive" culture that in many ways was as advanced as our own, if not more so.

Buried deep in the stacks of the Indiana library, my imagination went wild. As I turned the pages, the seeds were planted. Two years later I arrived in Alert Bay.

But then, after visits to the island, I saw that it was a far cry from what Curtis had pictured and the reports of Captain Cook and Franz Boas had told. It was evident that the high Kwakiutl culture of old, after the arrival of the white man, had diminished to an oppressive present tense.

Alert Bay, the center of the Kwakiutl Reserve on Cormorant Island, is a rough-and-tumble town: a mile-long oceanfront strip of bars, shabby hotels, grocery stores, marine supply stores, a post office, a bank, and the jail. In the middle of the strip is a small hospital and, next to it . . . the graveyard with vigilant totem poles. The doctor's name was Pickup. There used to be a judge named Deadman.

The town undertaker, Scuba (an avid diver), floated in and out of the bars saying, "Lookin' for business!" through a gap-toothed grin.

Even the town animals were hard-bitten. A big shaggy mongrel named Thor prowled the strip with a harem that included a couple sorry-looking yacht poodles that had jumped ship. The ever-present Alert Bay crows were a motley bunch: bent beaks, twisted toes, hoarse squawks. Stray cats were bone thin under huge outputs of fur.

It seemed forever raining and a chill wind knifed in off the bay, driving you to the closest source of warmth: The Nimpkish Bar, better known as "Bar None." No matter what time of day you wandered in, the place was packed with Kwakiutls, Swedes, Finns, Limeys mixing together, united by the need to forget the raw elements of fishing and logging for a while. A hard-core group of Indians had staked out a permanent corner for themselves and monopolized the pool table.

Tablecloths were blue towels, and the tiny round tables were packed solid with glasses as each man worked three or four beers at once. It was a dishonor to be the slightest bit pokey about buying a round. Men with faces that could split wood scoffed at the crazy cities down below. Weathered, creased hands lifted glasses. "It's head on here, but by gar, it's real!"

"Hey, Roy, you gettin' fat, or what?" one man hollered from across the room.

A big logger turned around on his seat, grabbing his ample belly. "I'm buildin' a shed over my tools!"

Going table to table were always a few Kwakiutl women with many sad stories: four or five kids by as many different fathers, spending their welfare checks on booze instead of properly feeding their babies. It didn't matter how unkempt they looked, how frazzled their lives—for in the beer parlors they were queens in the eyes of all the lonely, sloshed loggers.

As day dropped into night, a different type of drinking took place. Gone was the easygoing camaraderie. The serious drinkers came in (or continued from where they had been seated) to get down to business. I got the feeling that most of the Indians would have been just as happy if someone hit them between the eyes with a rubber mallet or etherized them. They were out to get totally numb.

The bartender told me, "Down south you have Wounded Knee. Here it's Bent Elbow."

A Kwakiutl woman, a reformed alcoholic and drug addict and a social worker of sorts, said, "It's bad in the Bay. The kids need to be out there like you. Not much trouble for them here. They see their fathers and mothers drunk all the time and they do no different. I went to white school and heard how America began with the pilgrims and how Indians are dirty savages. I tried to make it go away with booze and drugs, but it comes back worse. Then the white man says, see, I told you you were nothing but scum. I got pinched and did time and that got me respect from the kids on the street. It was a big deal because I was a criminal. It's hard on them here, but in Vancouver it's worse. They go there, steal for booze and smack money, girls whore. But not all kids. Some get out on their fathers' boats and fish and learn from the sea and animals like in the old days. A few make it through college and either join the system or come back and teach us how to speak the Big Meeting language— how to beat the white man his own way. But it's the lost ones that always make the news—the O.D.'s, suicides, dead-ends. The kids in the streets listen to me. They know where I been. I tell them where they're heading. Some stop, others just laugh, and . . . we end up crying for them."

* * *

At the west end of the mile-long strip of town, the Kwa-kiutls have their houses. The white people live on the hill-side above town or out on the east end. The Alert Bay taxi service runs the straight line—in both directions—stopping where pavement ends and woods take over.

One day, Malloff and I came into the bay for fuel and the mail, then he had to go out to the reserve to loan one of the Indian fishermen a tool he needed. Many of the Kwa-kiutls earned good livings as salmon fishermen. Industrious families, through generations of hard work, built up their own fleets of purse-seine boats.

It was a rare sunny day in Alert Bay, so we decided to walk out. As we stepped past the bars, drunk Indians popped out the door: "Hey, Malloff—come on—ready for you now!"

Malloff waved and kept walking. He was the unde-feated "Wrist Twister" of Alert Bay and it would take a new arm, fresh blood to put him down, as he had been through all the local challengers at least twice, whipping giant Indians who had a hundred pounds over him, but none with a thicker, quicker wrist than mighty Malloff.

Malloff saw the look of surprise on my face when we came to the Kwakiutl village. "What did you expect—they'd still be living in longhouses?" he said.

It was like suburbia, with split-level and ranch houses. Malloff knocked on a front door.

"It's open," a voice called.

We walked through a short hallway into the living room. Big Norm and his wife were sitting on a sofa eating Fanny Farmer chocolates while watching a soap opera on color television. There were porcelain knickknacks on the tables, blissful Hallmark Card scenes on the wall.

I couldn't believe it. It should be the way it was in Curtis, Cook, and Boas, but as I sank down into an easy chair and selected a chocolate turtle from the box Norm's wife offered, I conceded my last romantic hope for the "noble savage."

I asked if I could use the bathroom. After months of the outhouse, the flush toilet seemed so strange, so coldly efficient and closed in. I flushed it twice as if it were the first time I encountered the contraption. I was in a daze. . . . I had been in the bathroom longer than I was aware of.

"Thought you fell in!" Malloff said when I returned to the living room.

"I was . . . well, fascinated with the toilet—it flushes!"

Malloff laughed and laughed, understanding perfectly well—but the modern Indian couple looked at me as if I were a wild animal.

On the way back out to the island, I thought over how it has flip-flopped: Navajos wearing cowboy hats and boots, riding Ford Broncos, all the way to Kwakiutls watching *As The World Turns* and munching bonbons—while white men leave security to go back to the land, the wilder the better.

One night, while paddling the kayak home in thick fog, I saw a strange blue light hovering above, and now and then, amplified by the water, what sounded like laughter, a crowd of people laughing. I veered off course to check out the source of light and noise. Next thing I knew, I was staring into the barrel of a high-powered rifle.

"What da fuck!" a Kwakiutl said as he slowly lowered the gun. "Man, you come a cunt hair away from dyin'—sneakin' up on me like dat. I tout it was a whale or somefin'."

There was a tall can of Budweiser on the rail next to the Indian standing aboard a fishing boat. I saw through the cabin window that the blue light and noise were coming from a television set.

Though I was still shaking from the close call, I chuckled inside over the role reversals: white man in a canoe making his way home through the fog, while an Indian downs beer in front of the TV, quick on the draw when "danger" approaches.

As I paddled away, I heard an unforgettably shrill voice from the past. Whoever was aboard the *Big Chief* was watching *I Love Lucy*.

Then, a few days later, an Indian woman and her white husband asked, if they brought their two kids out, would I babysit them while they went away to Vancouver for the weekend? Sure. As it turned out, it wasn't "babysitting" at all. I learned from Conrad, eight, and Eva Crabe, twelve, that the child is, indeed, father to the man.

At first, worried about keeping them entertained, I suggested we go fishing in the dory to catch our supper. But, on the water, when I held out two handlines with cod jigs, Eva walked away to the front of the boat.

"Let's try for salmon," she said, peering down over the side.

"I've given up on salmon—haven't caught one in weeks. Come on—let's catch a big red snapper."

"But there's salmon here," she insisted.

"Oh, yeah, how do you know?"

She looked up at me with the dazzling force of sloe eyes, smooth brown skin, long blue-black hair—a woman at twelve years old. "Because I can see them," she slowly said.

Not being used to being around kids, I felt a bit miffed that my control, the upper hand, was slipping away. I looked over the side. "See—there's nothing but empty water. But okay, let's try."

I wasn't equipped for trolling, and with only one rod and reel aboard, I tied on a "buzz bomb" lure and handed the pole up to Eva. She cast smoothly and "mooched" the lure—imitating the irregular motions of an injured herring. As she reeled in, she sang a beautiful little song—something about calling the salmon to her, for she was now ready to eat them. I watched in amazement as she pulled in three salmon on her first three tries. She then handed me the pole.

I didn't catch any—because I hadn't expected to— and without a chant like Eva's I didn't stand a chance. I gave the pole to Conrad and he quietly pulled in two more "blue-backs"—baby coho—the sweetest meat imaginable.

In the kitchen, when I dropped the big frying pan into the airtight stove opening, Eva said, "Mike, you shouldn't fry them."

"Why not?"

"It burns the taste—cooks them too fast."

That suddenly made sense. "Well, what do you suggest?"

She smiled, lifted up the platter of fish, and went out the door. I followed along, feeling like a tenderfoot all over again.

Conrad already had a small fire going on the beach, and had placed various-sized sticks off to the side for Eva. Her ageless hands wove the sticks into upright grill holders that allowed the salmon meat to brown slowly around the smoky fire.

"Eva, where did you learn all this?"

"From my mum and grandmum. Our real home isn't Beaver Cove but on Mammallilacoola. That's where my mum was born on a fishnet."

There was cause for hope: traditions being passed down from grandmother to mother to Eva. . . . I learned of young people leaving the cities to return home to heal, ready to listen to the wisdom of their elders. There was a resurgence in the arts: totem poles being carved in new old ways; exciting, dynamic designs emerging in paintings, jewelry, hand-knit blankets and sweaters; young people taking the trouble to learn the mother tongue, revitalizing it in the process. A few students survived all the pitfalls, making it through college to become lawyers— helping their people win back rights in the courts, beating the white man at his own game. After decades of suppressing Kwakiutl culture, the Canadian government finally offered to return all the masks, robes, and artifacts confiscated from the outlawed Potlatches if the Kwakiutls would build a museum in Alert Bay. Once again, adzes and communal sweat shaped cedar pillars and planks into a longhouse treasure trove.

Of all the Kwakiutls I met, Basil Ambers best personified the new Indian. He struggled constantly with the paradox of living under the white man's rule, while trying to keep his heritage alive. Basil battled to win back Kwakiutl land rights from a greedy government. He formed councils, wrote a torrent of letters, faced big-shot bureaucrats with his mind loaded with ammunition compiled by Indian law students. Above all, when all else failed, Basil used his sense of humor.

The federal government paid a pittance for a bridge on the Kwakiutl Reserve. When Basil learned of the steal, he set up an armed blockade on the bridge. His plan was to tax all "white" vehicles until he had collected the amount the government paid, then send a check to Ottawa with NO DEAL printed across the top.

The driver of a bus carrying a high school band said, "We can't pay. I've just spent the last dollar on gas." Basil thought for a moment, then said, "Everybody out—with your instruments. Move it!"

As the musicians poured off the bus, he instructed them to line up out across the bridge. Basil played the moment for all it was worth. As he passed slowly in front of them in review, he saw from the kids' terror-struck expressions that they envisioned a "massacre at cross-creek."

"All right—now—to cross the bridge, your tax is one song—'This Land Is Your Land'—and we want to hear it good and loud!" The tubas lifted, trombones poised. . . .

In one hand, Basil lifted his rifle—striking up the band.

10

THE BOONDOCKS

There was much work to be done to beat the winter deadline—but it was as if I wanted the race to be close. Some days I dropped the axe to wander the beaches, combing the millions of stones for Indian artifacts. There was keen excitement in discerning a chipped edge, a sculpted curve—then picking it up and feeling the Kwakiutl past rush into you as you grasped a tool or weapon. From the Swanson Island beaches, Billy Proctor, the salmon fisherman, had started his extensive collection of ancient Kwakiutl tools. His prize finds were a canoe chisel and a pestle. As I wrapped my hands around the stone hammer, I felt the working hands of long ago. The island had been a Kwakiutl summer camp. While digging a new outhouse pit, I shoveled down through three feet of clamshell bits and, while checking each spadeful, discovered a spear tip carved from deer bone.

The Kwakiutls called the island Toulkwitla—"Place

143

of the Striped Rocks." Separating the beaches were slanted tables of rock shot through with broad veins of quartz and other minerals.

As I prowled the rocks and beaches, I examined the driftwood logs cast up by high tides. The logs were pock-marked from toredo worm attacks, polished smooth by the rasp of sand. They were bleached arboreal bones, tidal nomads. Some are international drifters. Old Hawaiian canoe carvers thanked their gods when the river-in-the-ocean brought them the pliable wood we know as cedar.

Frequent finds were logs with a logging company mark: initials and a grade number stamped into the butt end. Unlike branded cattle that break out of their pens, the logs didn't have to be returned to their owners. This beach-comber towed the strays home and fed them into the wood-stove.

If, upon arrival, the logs had wedged in the rocks or had rolled up out of reach of the following high tides, the wood became permanent fixtures on the island. It was these mainstays that once helped bring me home.

I was out in the dory jigging for cod early one evening when the outgoing tide swept the boat too fast over the holes. The fishing line streamed straight out across the surface, instead of dropping deep down. I decided to pack it in, head home; but then the outboard wouldn't start. While I tinkered with the motor, the swift tide carried the dory past the north end of the island. When I glanced up, my heart fell into my boots: north of Swanson was nothing but open ocean. I grabbed up the big oars and, standing upright in the midsection, pushed with all my fear. I had to think fast, compute all the factors. Darkness soon. A hundred yards offshore. No matches—a big blunder. "Always travel with fire in your pocket," Malloff had said how many times—but for this one instance my pretrip checklist wasn't all-inclusive. Without light I couldn't work on the engine once ashore, and to beach the boat and try to walk the mile home through the jungle in the dark would be mission near-impossible. As I punched with the oars, I weighed my two remaining choices: either spend a long, freezing night holed up in the woods, or fight home against the tide.

My arms stoked like pistons, pushing the dory through the four-knot surge. No moon and not one star. Thick cloud cover and the pitch-black night blotted out the island. I looked high and low, but couldn't even make out a tree shadow. I wanted to hug in along the island for security, but without visibility I couldn't risk hitting a rock pile.

I felt panic climb my spine. In the black night, without a landmark, I couldn't tell if I was overcoming the tide or being swept out to sea. But then I opened up the aperture, tilted my head back to be all eyes. I caught the glimmer of landlocked driftwood. Floating in darkness, the sun-bleached sticks pointed—in dot dashes—the way home.

The British Columbia coastal forests do not forgive the trespasses against them. Heavy rainfall buries past intrusions under ever-present growth. At first sight, from the lofty deck of a cruise ship, the Inside Passage looks untouched by man, but while hacking into the jungle, you may stumble across the cornerstone of an old monastery. On many islands I uncovered abandoned cabins, squeezing thick logs to spongy pulp in my hands. In back inlets, during autumn, I would go for hours along shores of dark evergreens, then suddenly would see a stand of alders, bright red—signaling second growth, and a settlement long since disappeared. In one place, the trees smashed up through a flimsy shack carrying away boards in branches. I found abandoned huts in a perfect circle, full of the feeling of failure, another utopia bottomed out (the site had changed—human nature hadn't). While traversing a far island, thinking, *Surely no one else has been here before,* I then

saw a tree lying down overly symmetrical. I slashed a ma-
chete through vines to gasp at a slew of ravens, bears,
human faces—classical Kwakiutl art—disintegrating into
the soil. And the abandoned sawmills and litter of logging
contraptions, metal dinosaurs being eaten alive by the undergrowth with no parts spared as pine duff soil applied its
acidity to erase the nuts and bolts of iron and steel that
flake away in your hands.

A favorite haunt was an abandoned cannery in Bones
Bay. The long, lofty building fronted an old Kwakiutl
graveyard where the smallpox-sick had been left to die. The
cannery was on its last legs as the sea ate the wood pilings
in jagged bites. With the tide away, the supporting stilts
stood as wavering, haphazard lines, seeming to be held
together by stubborn barnacles and clusters of mussels.
The building was engulfed by rain forest that spread thick
limbs over the rooftop. A great hush loomed around the
place. It was dripping in fog, haunted with history.

Between the cannery and the heap of soft bones was a
shanty, where, a half-century ago, Chinamen slept, ate,
and escaped their misery in the cloying embrace of opium.
Cut-glass vials turned up after a stormy sea raked the beach
beneath the hutch.

Stepping inside the shanty was like entering a time
warp. Chinamen long gone yet still visible. At first, I wondered why all the boxed shelves were stacked high up, but
when I peered inside I saw Chinese characters scripted
with penknives into the wood with a WONG, a LING carved,
here to stay, in plain English. I stood back and saw the
boxes for what they were—miniature bunks, no longer than
five feet and only a half turn across. I saw the bunk boxes
filled with Chinamen, one to a cubicle, like worker bees in
the hive, droning away the day of hard labor.

I clumped across the sagging floor to a side room that

served as the kitchen, with a smoke-black ceiling, a giant woodstove that fired the woks that cooked rice and fish, which fueled the workers to withstand the demanding cannery. Their bustling energy hovered—palpable human vibrations outlasting wood in the corrosive sea air.

I left the China hutch and walked through the cannery, my footfalls echoing throughout the deserted mausoleum. The immense space was empty save for neat piles of purse-seine nets now in winter storage. Nets that poured off big drums, hauling heavy money out of Blackfish Sound in the summer—now hibernating, landlocked under the protective roof. But as I fingered the fine mesh, I thought of all the salmon tons that had been processed in here year after year. For men to build so big so far away, there had to be a reason, a return on their investment. That there was. The fish were many and so were the Chinamen, who worked for little. A dollar a day was their pay.

The salmon were dumped out on long tables, where head, tail, and fins were cut off and the entrails removed with a few flashing strokes of a knife. The dressed fish were then passed into tanks of fresh water, where another team stripped off the scales; then came a final dunking in brine tanks to thoroughly wash the meat.

With one stroke of six-bladed gang knives, Chinamen divided the salmon into large sections, then cut the pieces lengthways into strips, which quick hands packed tightly into cans. Tops were fitted and soldered on, the full cans submerged in vats of boiling water to create a seal and kill germs. They were final-inspected for leaks, labels were lacquered on, then they were packed in boxes and shipped out to cities down along the coast.

The Chinese labor was supplied by a contracting firm based in Vancouver, which made an agreement with the canning company to oversee all the work at a fixed price per case—a system favored by the cannery owners, for then all they had to concern themselves with was delivering the fish and then counting their profits.

But the Chinese rebelled against the cramped housing and inadequate sanitary conditions. By 1935, unionization of the cannery workers improved their lot. But then a few years later the Chinamen were replaced by a mechanical device, the Smith Butchering Machine, better known as the "Iron Chink." With machines working nonstop to increase production, the product itself disappeared. Boom went belly-up as the great mass of salmon dwindled, and the backwater canneries closed.

I wandered over to the shanty for another look. As I passed the bunks with the charactered graffiti, I wondered where, from here, all the Chinamen went. Some probably returned to the homeland, having had their fill of America, with many others sending for their families to then seek good fortune in Vancouver's Chinatown—the second largest such settlement on the coast.

I stopped to look out a window, the glass rippled with age. The tide was in full. I gazed down into the water shimmering cold and clear, with red, rubbery starfish draped over deep rocks; the open, white petals of feeding anemones; flags of seaweed fluttering in the currents; herds of small fish pulsing the way a heart sends blood through veins.

I recognized the scene as unchanged from what the Chinamen had seen. They could lose themselves deep in the undertow of opium simply by eye-gliding through the underwater world out in front of them. Far from home, numb from work, and rattled at night by unburied Indians, the workers sought reasons to keep going through forms of escape.

I walked to a back corner. Scattered across the floor

were outboard engine parts, dull saw blades, busted stove pieces: the detritus that litters cold-coast buildings. But shining up through the slag and dross were the heavenly bodies of Rita Hayworth and Hedy Lamarr—torn from the pages of *Life*—fallen from cubicle walls.

Out in the boondocks, inspiration dies hard.

11

THE PERFECT TURKEY

Our nearest neighbor was the caretaker of Berry Island, four miles away. His name was Alec Stuart, retired logger.

The day before Thanksgiving, Alec came by in his skiff for a visit. After coffee and the usual discussions of weather and fishing, Alec asked if I wanted to go back with him: "It's just that, well . . . um . . . be good to have some company over the holidays." His old logger's face flushed an embarrassed red at having revealed his loneliness.

"Alec, I'd be happy to come over. I'll get my sleeping bag."

"And tomorrow, you and Beth come by," he said to Malloff. "I bought a big turkey in Alert Bay. I'll cook 'er up and then we'll have the holiday all together, eh?" Malloff and Beth quickly accepted, and a party mood animated our departure.

After I'd stowed my pack and myself in the bow of the

151

boat, Alec pushed off the beach and hopped in, starting the outboard engine. As conversation was impossible over the loud drone, we silently shared the splendor of the unspoiled expanses. The evergreen mountains looming over the crystal and slate sea were dusted halfway down with fresh snow. The blue sky, inflated with great clarity, shared its immensity with both the setting sun and the sparkling of Venus as we approached the landing at Berry Island.

After securing the boat to the dock, Alec showed me through the one-story house—four rooms behind the long kitchen that fronted the sea. The back rooms were closed off behind heavy doors. Most of the year, Alec lived in the warmer kitchen/bedroom. Like most Inside Passage houses, there was one room roughed out in plywood, a future den or workshop. But for now, Alec's den was crammed with bulk food, an odd lot of framed windows, piles of chain saw and outboard engine parts, shelves of wallpaper rolls, paint cans, and assorted interior fixtures. The detail work had obviously been postponed for a rainy day, but was never finished because, ironically, it rained all the time.

A top shelf was lined with paperback books; half were Louis L'Amour westerns and the other group, gothic romances. It was difficult to imagine the big logger appreciating equally *Mustang Man* and *Ecstasy Supreme*. However, Alec explained that a visiting yacht on its way to Alaska had dropped off a box of books that had been read that year by the owners, who had intended to donate them to the Alert Bay Library but, upon seeing that Alec was starved for reading material, left the books with him instead. Thus, the Berry Island branch of the Alert Bay library was born.

A stack of chores requiring the efforts of two men took us outside for some heavy lifting, moving, swearing, and smashed fingers before we finally sat down at the kitchen table, beside a window overlooking the sea, to engage in conversation and storytelling—such a luxury in that isolated world. We started drinking a little rum in our coffee, then a little coffee in our rum, then dispensed with coffee entirely. The rum was "Navy O.P.," at 120 (over) proof, as dark as spar varnish, and tasted as bitter as it looked.

"Alec, how did you ever end up out here?"

"I'm on probation," he replied. "Had to find a place where I'd stay out of trouble. Sure ain't much of that around here." He paused to wave his coffee mug at the sea. "The only visitor I have is the tide. . . ."

"What happened—what did you do?"

"Oh, a buddy and I were in a bar in Hope, British Columbia, mindin' our own business, when this young Mountie decides my friend is some escaped fugitive, and, of course, the Mounties always get their man. So when this kid pulled out his pistol, I grabbed it, pushed it against his face, and broke his nose. Hell, I was sixty-nine years old, but did time in the pen for assaulting a lawman half my age. Ha!

"When I first went in, the guy taking fingerprints grabbed my hands and whistled. Said he'd been there twenty-five years and never seen a pair as big. He registered my hands as lethal weapons. I was North American Golden Gloves champ back in 1927 at a hundred and seventy-five pounds.

"I was brought up in the bush, the Caribou country. Went off to New York City, Madison Square Garden, in cowboy boots and a ten-gallon hat. But that's another story."

Noticing a beautiful old fiddle hanging up on the wall, I asked, "Do you play?" He nodded, gazing out the window at the last glow of light on the horizon.

"Started when I was a kid. Out in the Caribou there'd be dances every now and then, and they were big get-togethers 'cause that's the few times when folks from all around got together. Everybody'd hitch up their team and ride the buckboard to wherever the dance was. Some came fifty, sixty miles through the snow. All the men brought bottles of home brew and stashed 'em out in the snowbanks. I sat up in the hayloft with a young pretty and then went down to play the fiddle. I could really twirl the skirts!"

"Play some now, Alec," I said.

"Aw, come on, you don't wanna hear an old geezer."

"Play."

"You're sure? Okay."

He stood up, tucked the butt of the fiddle under his square chin, and picked up the bow. His massive hand swooped and dipped like a bird in flight. Alec's face transformed as he watched the bow fly across the fiddle, rendering "Down Yonder," "Turkey in the Straw," "Heel Toe Polka," "Ragtime Annie," and "Life in the Finland Woods." The whirling rhythms evoked barn dances, as well as farms, ranches, and burly logging camps—all danced their way into Alec's island kitchen through his music. His fiddle made my feet twitch, my hands clap; I hollered and cried, moved to tears by this folk music so alive that it seemed to stir every passion.

Alec turned back to the window, nodding to the water as he sawed, and the tide seemed to slap in time against the pilings as he dipped his head—his white hair and green eyes a foil to the rosewood fiddle—and finished with a vigorous glissando.

Later, our talk traveled out to sea, with Alec reminiscing about a salmon-trolling boat he'd rigged for big tuna off the west coast of Vancouver Island. We then started in on the second bottle of rum. . . . The discussion moved on to women, and our talk ambled far into the night in that direction.

Suddenly, it was daylight. I awoke on the bed against

the kitchen wall. My head felt unstable and potentially explosive. I was nearly frozen with cold.

"Alec," I whispered.

My utterance produced no response, so I inhaled deeply, trying not to upset the precarious equilibrium in my head, then yelled, *"Alec!"*

No answer. After the shock waves from those syllables subsided in my head, I slid to the floor and crawled into the living room.

Alec was comatose on the couch and could not be aroused. The whole house was freezing and the fuel box empty. I staggered outside to the chopping block. Each time I managed to hit a wood chunk with the ax, the contact reverberated inside my throbbing head, but finally I had enough wood split to get a fire going in the kitchen stove. While thawing out next to the heat, I noticed the clock.

"Alec," I yelled, "the turkey—shouldn't we be doing something with the turkey? They'll be here in a few hours!"

One bloodshot eye fluttered open. "Wha-ho-kay, but jesss—" He resumed snoring. I checked the rum bottles on the kitchen table. One was empty and the other three-quarters gone. Between trips to a window for fresh air to clear my head and trips to the stove to try to get warm, I evaluated the damage. Alec had kept a couple of cups ahead of me, so he would have to sleep longer before he'd be of any use. I covered him with my down sleeping bag and gingerly made my way back to the kitchen.

On the counter was a stark white turkey, huddled there so big and raw and naked that it was hard to imagine it transformed into something edible. But guests were coming and the challenge galvanized me: a hangover was no excuse for reneging on a dinner invitation—especially on Thanksgiving—and with Malloff's gargantuan appetite.

I searched the cupboards. There was one spiral-ringed book slumped in a corner. I blew off the dust: *A Guide for The Homemaker,* circa 1926. I consulted the index, but when I turned to the cooking section, specifically "Turkey," most of the page appeared to have been shredded. Mice. I could read, however, the following: "—each pound for 15 minutes at a constant temperature of 350°."

Grabbing the thick turkey legs and lifting, I calculated, "About twenty pounds. . . . Alec, we just might make it."

Digging out a giant pan, I plopped the turkey into position and slid it into the oven. As I fed a steady stream of wood into the stove, I wondered about the stuffing and recalled seeing a big can of bread crumbs—yes, on top of the chicken coop. I retrieved it and poured all the crumbs into a mixing bowl.

Back at the stove, I checked the temperature gauge recessed in the oven door. The needle was swinging back and forth, sweeping all the degrees. I fed in more wood, hoping to stabilize the temperature, but the needle slammed past 500 degrees, quivering in the red zone. I flapped the door open and shut to cool the bird. The scanty instructions scolded, "at a constant temperature of 350°." I added the cookbook to the flames.

So, each time I added wood, I counterbalanced the initial blast of heat by flapping the door open and shut, and decided to ignore the temperature gauge, as it made my head ache. The juice gathering at the bottom of the pan triggered a reflex action, so I grabbed a big spoon and lifted the juice up over the sides of the bird. The skin gradually began to assume a golden glow.

Into the bowl of bread crumbs, I cracked two eggs, added a dash of cinnamon, a bit of nutmeg, a handful of raisins, all sorts of herbs, and—why not?—poured in the remaining rum. After packing this mixture into the cavity of the turkey, I continued my guessing game: the ingredients of gravy.

I mixed whole-wheat flour in with the pan drippings. At least the result was the right color: brown. I tossed a salad and covered it with a cold, wet towel.

Alec revived, looking like seven brands of purgatory. "Oh, you got 'er goin'," he said, as if it were quite natural to wake up on Thanksgiving to find a houseguest commanding the kitchen. "I'm gonna wash up," he said, shuffling away and disappearing before I could ask his advice on anything.

Hearing the approaching hum of Malloff's speedboat, I hurriedly cleared the mess, tried to spruce myself up, set the table, said a brief prayer, swore off rum forever, and put out the gravy and salad.

Malloff, Beth, and Alec all arrived at about the same time. Alec was freshly shaved, combed, and wearing a clean shirt. Just as everyone settled into chairs, I pulled the turkey out of the oven and handed Alec the carving knife; he sliced according to requests.

Malloff forked a chunk of meat into his mouth. As he chewed, his eyes brightened. "Perfect," he said. "Crisp skin and the meat is moist. Damn, this is *good*!" And he was right. To my astonishment, the turkey was excellent. Superb. The best I'd ever tasted!

"And the dressing, what *flavors*," Beth said as her eyes moved back and forth from Alec to me.

"The boy did it all," Alec said graciously, looking up from his plate and helping himself to more turkey.

"Michael, you did all of this—and in that oven?" asked Beth.

"Yeah, no sweat." I shrugged, and nonchalantly discussed the fine points of cooking on a woodstove, suggesting a few staples which might have allowed a more epicurean spread.

With the stuffing served on our plates, Malloff abruptly ended my charade of master chef.

"What the hell's this?" he asked as he poked the serving fork into the bird's cavity and extricated the package of giblets.

After the laughter quieted, Alec regaled them with our earlier festivities, and I recounted my astonishing luck in the kitchen.

Never before were so many thanks given to such a perfect turkey!

12

═══〜〜〜═══

UNDERWATER

F eeling somewhat limited, contained by the island, from
a local diver I bought equipment to explore underwater.

The rubber wetsuit was my passkey to a new world. I
was able to step off the island and fly free through the sea.

At first, I shuddered as the forty-two-degree water
seeped in against my skin, the cold squeezing my head like
a steel band. After a half minute, body heat warmed the
water and tense muscles relaxed as I drifted through the
fluid world. As I soared out through the blue, my mind
eased into the alpha cycle and elusive abstracts shaped
themselves into cognizant ideas. Glass mask like a camera
lens, I filmed all in my path, with the soundtrack a boom-
ing heart and lungs like cavernous bellows.

I usually went in at slack tide—an hour gap between
high and low when the currents were limp. If I was early or

late, the dives were impeded by coursing water. I didn't fully realize the power of the tide until, one day, I rode it.

I entered the sea as it started to pull away from the beach—keeping my arms in against my sides, hands flat on my thighs. I held the finned feet together and used them as a rudder—swiveling my ankles to tack in the current. Near the surface, visibility was limited. The sea was a soup of plankton, algae, and silt from the island's raging creeks. As the minuscule particles streamed by my face mask, I felt less a solid entity and more a smattering of molecules.

I slithered down through a bed of kelp, the thirty-foot fronds fluttering like streamers in the wind. Down . . . down . . . I curvetted like a dolphin. The water cleared as I sailed over a meadow of weeds bent and trembling in the flow; then I was alongside an immense rock wall covered with goose barnacles. From each parted beak, two cirri waved back and forth, sweeping in diatoms. Triggered by the uniform rhythm, the opening movement of Beethoven's "Pastoral" symphony washed across my mind. It was pure rapture, hearing the verdant music conducted by the multitude of tiny wands! I spread-eagled against the tide, trying to stay the magic moment . . . but the force swept me on.

I soared out over a field of white anemones, their tendrils seductively enticing small fish. I grabbed hold of a jutting rock and examined a cluster of mussels: blue shells spangled with bright silver. Feeling my lungs starting to strain, I curved my back and ascended, up to the wavering ceiling . . . puncturing water, gaining air. Through the snorkel tube, I blew out the expended breath and sucked in fresh life.

I dove, kicking down, meeting again the even push of the tide. I spotted a group of tommy cod below—a flight of arrows straight off the bow. I turned on my side and gazed over a half acre of sea urchins: strawberry cockleburs covering the rocky ledges.

I snatched up a sun-star by a leg, flung it out ahead like a Frisbee, then dove under and kept tipping it up with one finger as it sank. I then pulled in my gloved finger and watched the bright sun sink away into the abyss.

I shot upward and spouted like a whale—attached to the surface by the need to breathe. I sucked air in deep and then sounded. Sensing movement behind, I spun around smack into a cloud of fish that parted, rippling around me . . . suspending time . . . making reality a dream. I was in a tunnel of silver streaks with dots of ink-black eyes, thousands of surreal eyes dot-dashing by on metallic flumes. I looked up and down. Continuous walls of movement shimmered around me. The creation appeared endless, but then, abruptly, the water was clear.

I spun around. The sea was vacant of fish. I wondered if it had been a hallucination, but then I saw the soft rain and lifted my black-gloved hands through fluttering silver scales. The tide moved me on. Behind the oval window, salt tears wet my face. I was overwhelmed with awe. How fortunate, humbled, I felt to experience such wonders. Frescoes of herring—living art!

I thought of Picasso's axiom that "Art is a lie that enables us to see the Truth." I thought of Nature as the Truth.

I rode the tide the length of the island, and then crawled out onto land—all my weight returning in gravity's hold. As I trudged begrudgingly over the rock piles back to home, I thought of how the word *tide* translates as "time"— high and low—tick-tock the pendulum swings in the hand of man the measurer. "Tide and time wait for no man," the old proverb says. But out in the flowing sea itself, all demarcations cease to be. In the ocean, you never know what

century it is. Bathed in eternity, the weightless diver soars
out beyond measure.

The forests aren't limited to land. The sea grows abundant
stands of foliage that tower over the floor. A favorite underwater activity was climbing through the kelp forests. I
sipped a deep breath and followed a stipe down hand-over-
fist as far as my lungs would allow. The thin trunks can
extend as long as 150 feet to the sea bottom. Kelp anchor
themselves to rocks with grips that resemble tree roots; and
just as rodents and other small creatures make their dens
under forest trees, the brittle star, miniature urchins, and
sea worms crowd in under the kelp root arches, sheltered
from heavy weather and hungry predators.

I released the stipe and floated up into the canopy of
fronds. They wrapped around me like boa constrictors: the
harder I thrashed, the tighter they wound. I reached to my
shin for my knife, slashing a way out. A Kwakiutl fisherman told me that if a sea otter is being pursued by a killer
whale, it heads full-tilt toward a kelp patch and flings itself
into the middle. The whale halts, fearing imprisonment.

The Indians referred to kelp as the "Mother of the
Sea," for it is on her skirts that herring lay their millions of
eggs. The Kwakiutls used to dry the long stipes that washed
ashore, making resilient fishing line. Astute fishermen know
that kelp fronds indicate the direction in which the tide and
fish are flowing. Kelp also provides a survival food. Chop
off the youngest frond, roll it into a tube, and slice it thin.
Boil these noodles, and you have a very nutritious kelp
spaghetti.

As I snorkeled along the shoreline, I often flopped onto
land to study the tide pools. Shallow ocean was trapped in
rock basins. Bright green seaweed lined the walls; anem-

ones, sea slugs, hydroids, mussels, starfish resided in the warm pools.

I stared in fascination at one pool where still water was blue sky, and the various creatures resembled flowers, trees, hills, houses. The enchanting world in miniature made me wish I could shrink to fit, become Lilliputian instead of being overgrown Gulliver.

My favorite pool was in a jagged fissure. I found it just after discovering the pictograph of the "human killer whale" on the base of a cliff. I stepped up out of the kayak onto a narrow ledge to examine the pictograph close up. I then followed the ledge around the brunt of the cliff. It led into a hollow chamber just above the sea. There in the rock floor was a slash-shaped tide pool. The small cavern was open at the top. The pool shook sunlight into shimmering patterns on the walls.

One night, I felt the tide pool calling. I paddled over in the baidarka. The tide had barely retreated from the ledge. I held the kayak's long leash and inched past the guardian pictograph, which looked fierce in the narrow beam of my flashlight. I then killed the lamp. The hollow chamber glowed with an eerie, flickering light. For an instant I thought someone was within, but the light didn't appear man-made. I crept in . . . and gasped in astonishment. The jagged fissure held coruscating phosphorescence: a bolt of pure lightning pulsed across the rock floor.

I felt myself progressing into a retroactive state of mind. Since I was free of the confinement of time and obligations, I felt the impulsive child reemerge, shrugging off the somber adult, being magnetized to magic: seeking out the heightened moments.

As a boy when I went to the circus I was enthralled with the trapeze act. Watching men "fly through the air with the greatest of ease" convinced me that someday I would run off to the Big Top and become a trapeze flier. I even had my name all polished: "Barzini the Birdman."

Religiously, every Saturday, I went to the movie theater to watch Tarzan fly through his jungle on his network of vines. Dad tied a thick rope to a beam in the hayloft ceiling at our farm. For hours I glided back and forth above the straw hills.

When I played football, I was the end, split out away from the heaving goliaths. My skills were speed and spring, enabling me to soar up above the clash to catch the ball, advance our effort.

I love the earth, but not as I do the sea and sky. To the earth I feel the dutiful love of a son for his mother. The sea and sky are Sirens who entice me. Mother Earth is most beautiful, but I rebel against her attachment—her gravity hold. No leap ever lasts long enough.

I came to see people of the earth as ponderous heavyweights. The farmers and miners I knew; Brueghel's peasants, van Gogh's "Potato Eaters" seem to have earth for flesh, stones for bones. Their beauty is overstated in the very statement of their forms. They lack the counterpoint of flexibility and finesse. They leave deep footprints.

The most beautiful forms to me are those of dancers, matadors, gymnasts, birds, and fish. The ultimate design is when there is nothing left to take away.

When I piloted a plane, I felt let down. I wasn't flying: a raucous engine flew me. I tried hang gliding but the wings still weren't mine. During my first snorkel dive in Freshwater Bay, I finally flew free. In the sea I found my sky.

When asked about his fascination for diving, Jacques Cousteau replied: "It's weightlessness. It's the only element in which you forget gravity. Since we are born we are crushed on land by our weight. We are bearing that burden until we die. To me, it's the origin of the concept of original sin. When the first vertebrates crawled out of the sea, that was the original sin."

Standing on the beach covered in rubber blubber, a wall-eyed mask, finned feet, chunks of lead on a belt for ballast, I felt like a giant groper out of water, clumsily flip-flopping over land—but once afloat, I felt the exultation of a released prisoner.

I learned that moving underwater is a world apart from moving on land. As if in a slow-motion dream, the slightest effort propels you an amazing distance. During my first attempt, I fought through the water with flailing arms and legs; with gravity's resistance suddenly gone, I eventually saw how forceful I *didn't* need to be. When I relaxed, let go, I swam with the effortless ease of the fish.

To test my swimming, I would approach a school of rock cod. If my movements were smooth and flowing, I could, at times, get close enough to touch them. If there was tension in my body, if my motion was forced, the fish darted out in a tangled pattern, an external show of knotted nerves.

Fish have a sensitive lateral line along their flanks which receives pressure waves informing them of the approach of friend or foe, and the "radar" line also picks up prey. A sick or wounded fish shudders spastically, sending out choppy signals that trigger an attack response in predators. Sharks have extremely sensitive receivers. From miles away, they can pick up distress signals and track them unerringly to the source. We regard the shark as a ruthless butcher, when it is merely the efficient effect of the cause: the weak ending their lives by quickly disturbing, altering the grid pattern—calling in sure death out of the blue.

Most sharks avoid the North Pacific due to the frigid temperature. However, the diver must watch that his actions don't bring out the wolf eel or lingcod. Wolf eels make their homes in rock crannies; shy by nature, they will attack only if surprised or provoked. If a diver happens to poke his hand into a lair, the coiled six-foot wolf eel may spring out like a jack-in-the-box, delivering a fierce bite. With powerful jaws and razor-sharp fangs, it can easily shear fingers off a hand.

The lingcod, like the barracuda, is territorial. The male guards the eggs and will attack an intruder. An unaware Blackfish Sound diver lost part of his scalp to a big eighty-pound lingcod.

At times, the sea lion can pose a danger. One diver was the recipient of a cow's amorous advances. She made brazen passes at him, rolling her curvaceous self against him and delivering love "pats" with her flippers. After she stripped off his mask, the diver ended the engagement by madly waving his arms and exhaling a storm of bubbles.

While snorkeling, I surprised a sunbathing seal, stretched out on the edge of a small islet. I came up and unintentionally spouted directly alongside of it. The seal leapt clear over me, splashing in. Facedown, I hadn't seen it—until it shattered the water beside me. Fear exploded throughout my body until the image-flash registered in my brain. I then sipped a quick breath and went down after it. But the seal seemed to free-fall, as if dropping down an elevator shaft. Its ovoid shape became attenuated, squeezed by the increasing pressure. A brown line became a dash, then a dot that disappeared into the deep. In a few seconds, it had descended a hundred feet.

Seals can go down as deep as 1,500 feet and stay submerged for a half hour on a single breath. They have one and a half times the blood of a land mammal of similar size, and upon diving, a seal's heart slows from 150 beats a minute to just 10 pulses.

When the seal surfaces it only requires a few breaths to replenish its oxygen debt. Its lungs are slightly larger than a man's, but unlike man, the seal can empty and refill almost completely with each breath. When a scuba diver ascends too rapidly to the surface, the nitrogen from his air supply forms bubbles of gas in his blood vessels. The seal avoids the bends by taking in very little air when diving, and exhales as it goes under, with blood and muscles acting as built-in "tanks" storing the majority of oxygen.

As I stared down into the depths, the diving seal reappeared in my mind's eye. I thought of how limited man's powers are compared to the animals'. Perhaps that is why we kill them.

In *Toilers of the Sea,* Victor Hugo wrote: "The octopus, O horror inhales a man. It draws him to itself and into itself, and bound, immovable, he feels himself slowly ingested by that incredible being which is the monster. The terrible tentacles are supple as leather, solid as steel, cold as night."

Brainwashed by the chilling rhetoric of Hugo and Jules Verne, I felt an odious repulsion for the "devilfish." The two creatures people fear most are the snake and the spider. I regarded the octopus as a combination of both. When I learned that the largest octopuses in the world live in the British Columbia waters, for a time I was reluctant to dive—or fish.

Malloff enjoyed telling the story of a logger who bought a new wooden rowboat. Before the maiden voyage, the woodsman brought aboard his third arm—an ax—handy for getting a bite in a drifting log. After breaking a bottle of beer over the bow, the logger rowed out to try a new cod hole. He dropped his lure over the side and played out the line. Raising the lure off the bottom, he felt a strong tug and fought to haul the line in hand over fist. Suddenly a huge tentacle grabbed the gunwale while another arm slithered in behind and wrapped around the man's ankle. Six more arms came up swinging over the side. The logger grabbed his ax, wildly chopping the tentacles—and his brand-new boat—to bits.

A local diver told me: "No need to worry if you bump into one—they're shy creatures. But some of them will let you dance 'em around. Hold them out arm's length, and that way they won't get ahold of you. If it does slip an arm around you, relax. Don't yank away. That arm can be like a noose—the more you pull, the tighter it gets."

I cautiously continued my diving, planning on keeping my distance. Waltzing a giant octopus around in my arms was not my idea of a swinging good time.

I first sighted one when I had gone down thirty feet to pluck a few sea urchins from the top of a boulder. As I started my ascent, out of the corner of the mask I saw what appeared to be a snake or eel. After getting air, I dropped back down behind the boulder. Feeling secure, I looked over the top. Hidden away in its rock-wall lair, an octopus was waving a slender white arm through clear water. The motion was hypnotic as suction cups rippled consecutively over the tentacle flowing back and forth.

That night I read in a Cousteau book that the octopus waves an arm, oftentimes, to lure a crab. After capturing the crab, with its beak the octopus cracks the crustacean open, and then the flexible tips of its arms pry into even the smallest joints of the crab's legs, passing the meat from sucker cup to cup, up to the beak.

The next morning, I dove back in, searching for the lair. No cave or large cavity. There was a fissure splitting the rock wall, but I passed it off as being too narrow to house a giant octopus. But there on the ledge fronting the crack was a crab shell, intact except for a jagged hole on the underside, and also an empty abalone shell. I quickly kicked back a few yards, not wanting to be added to the collection.

I surfaced and waddled up across the rocks to cut off a branch from a cedar tree. I had read that the Greeks lure octopuses out of their lairs by waving an olive branch in front of them. I was still afraid, but the only way I've found to overcome fear is to call it out and face it directly.

I floated down above the lair and waved the cedar fronds. . . . No show of octopus. I slowly slid the branch into the fissure, expecting it to be yanked from my hand—but the stick tapped against solid rock. I finally got up enough nerve to place my mask against the crack and peer in: empty darkness.

When I dove down to the lair the following day, I tried the waving branch again with no results. I looked in—still empty. Out of air, I soared up top. When I glanced down to direct my descent, I saw the octopus, about fifty yards away. It was enormous—at least eight feet long—but it moved as gently as a billowing scarf, the long tentacles gathered in perfect spirals.

As it moved it changed colors. Over rocks it showed gray mottled pink. In a field of weeds it grew bright green. The octopus then slowed and settled down onto the empty bottom like a parachute. I watched closely as it touched down, but then lost the creature as it composed a precise match to the brindled floor. I kicked down a couple body lengths. Black pupils shifted up; the octopus flushed red and sped away. I swam fast, trying to stay close, my fear overpowered by fascination. Approaching the lair, its body stretched rubber thin, then slipped all at once into the crevice!

I told no one of the octopus. It was regarded by many islanders as fine food, and I had heard of divers driving them out of their lairs by pouring in copper sulfate. Demented amusement, watching the "monsters" writhe in agony. I knew of a diver who had made a pet of one. Not only did he dance with it, but hand-fed it as well. Torturing or pampering the octopus was not what I had in mind.

While going about my day topside on the island, I felt satisfaction just knowing that such an astonishing creature existed—gracing the ocean, and only a few yards away. It was as if because of the octopus I could now extend beyond myself in a different form, experience life in a richer way because the animal within me created another plane, new points of intersection.

13

CLEAR THE WAY

The oars stroked the water—back and forth—again and again. No past or future, no memories or expectations. I pushed the skiff through the night sea.

A flash of light—a fish skipped across the surface. High above, the mewing of a gull.

The sunset glowed crimson above the mountain ridge. White flecks of spume freckled the sea. I dabbed a finger in the froth and touched it to my tongue, tasting forest.

Under tusks of moon, Swanson Island loomed like a hairy mammoth. I looked up across the mass of trees that formed the dark pelage. A prominent humped back showed my destination.

Low in the island's shadow was a white beach, a flat mirror reflecting faint moonlight. I kept the luminescence centered between my fists, pushing the oars until the light bent around me. The skiff slid over remnant clamshells, left by Indians, crushed by ocean. I stepped out, grabbed the bow, and dragged the boat up under the skirt of a cedar tree.

I scuffed a hole into the shell sand, picked up a drift-wood stick, and whittled kindling. I pinched the shavings together in the divot and struck a match. As the curls flamed, I added small sticks, creating a hollow of warmth in the cold night.

From the skiff I took out a jug of water, a cooking pot, and a fish. I then went in search of a Kwakiutl "grill." I grabbed a dead branch lying under the tree and split it along its length—clean through—with my knife. I filleted the cod and placed the slabs of fish in between the two wood halves, then poked thin twigs horizontally through the fillets to keep them extended. With kelp stipe, lying nearby, I wrapped together the two ends of the stick.

I jabbed the bottom of the grill into the sand on the other side of the low fire, and sat back watching the meat brown in the heat and smoke.

After I ate, I filled the pot with water and set it down on the fire. When the water rolled, I tossed in a handful of spruce needles. As the tea steeped, I thought of how it is worth pushing yourself to exhaustion just to feel the release of a tired body warmed simultaneously by fire and food.

A few quick sips of tea, and then I pulled the skiff behind the trunk of a tree. I took out the sleeping bag and unrolled it alongside the boat. I slid in, creating warmth. I burrowed deep into the bag . . . drifting away. . . .

Hooting, an owl cut into my dream. I sat up, breaking the seal of warmth in the bag, crawling out into the cold twilight. As I picked up sticks, I tried to recall the dream, but my mind was frozen solid.

After reviving by the fire, I walked out across the beach. The flat water mirrored pale light. A blue heron on stilt legs stood still on a drifting log, peering down into the water, long beak poised to stab.

I knelt at the edge of the sea, cupped my hands, and slapped cold water against my face. Walking back to the fire, I saw jets of water spurt up from the sand. With my hands I dug out a dozen clams. I shelled them and then skewered the ragged meat on a sharp stick.

As the clam-kabobs roasted over the fire, I watched winter finally establish itself—but with such timid light. The north wind, however, arrived very sure of itself. I held my hands out over the boiling pot; spruce steam prickled my palms.

As I ate, I studied the cedar tree I had slept under. The trunk started straight up but then turned into a torso of fossilized muscles with twists and curls showing tenacity in wood. The tree had spent its life fighting. Many of its opponents had steamrolled clear across Canada, and in passing had blasted the old hobgoblin that dug in with root toes while crooked back and arms did battle.

I thought of how we date a tree by adding up its rings. But counting doesn't give a true summation. The gnarled cedar never bothered with birthdays, and neither should we. If the tree knew how old it was, it would have keeled over long ago. Life should be regarded as one long year aged by many seasons: it is the experiences, the storms we weather that measure us—not the numerical turn of a calendar decreed by some distant Caesar.

I flopped the skiff over, covering my gear. I looked out across the beach. Small waves broke and foaming tongues lapped at my footprints. I turned and went in under the trees.

Waves of air roared in the tall treetops. The sun rained down through holes in the canopy. Just as the bolts of light touched the floor, they were snuffed by the closing branches. The strobe effect danced everything solid into motion.

Across the forest floor sprawled a vast crisscross of toppled cedars and firs. Seeing that it would be a slow go through the mass of timber, I decided to climb a steep bluff that sided the tree graveyard. I took off my hiking boots and socks, stuffed the rag wool into the boots, and tied them up by their laces to back belt loops. I relied on the finest climbing implements ever made: fingertips and toes found minuscule holds in the cold rock. I ascended.

I struggled to silence the top-of-the-head voice that clamored, *You're out of your mind—toes can't fit in there! What if you get halfway up and there are no holds, huh? Then what?* I flashed back to the time I tried to climb a tree on my twenty-first birthday: the static was so overwhelming that I hugged a high limb and froze.

As a boy I had lived in the treetops. The child's mind is calm, for he "thinks" with his body; the adult's body is blocked by worried interference.

Fingers and toes reached, gripped, pushed. Once it bit its tongue, the analytical brain actually enjoyed the ride.

On top of the granite bluff was a dwarf pine tree. Its roots had cleaved the rock open, searching for sustenance within the firmament. I pushed against the squat tree. It pushed back.

I rubbed warmth into my toes, put on the socks and boots, and continued up a steep hillside. Open space between trees and rocks. Chalky light. Blue shadows.

Snow fell. I looked up into the open belly of a cloud. The wind was gone. The flakes drifted straight down, stirring in my mind the Zen adage: "No snowflake ever falls in the wrong place."

My breathing seemed amplified in the still, chill air. As I climbed in a short-step rhythm, I thought of the Buddhist monks who live in mountain monasteries. Besides uniting their souls with the scenery, they are on intimate terms with the wildlife, so much so that in some sects when a monk dies his body is left out in the forest for the animals to devour.

I recalled that the Zen masters are known by the name of the mountain they live and teach on. The Oxhead master, Tao Lin, built a nest in a tall treetop for his meditation. Sitting up in it, he once had a conversation with a government official. "Isn't it dangerous up there?" the politician asked. "Where you are is far more dangerous," Tao Lin replied.

The slope grew steeper. Leg muscles cramped, breath came in gaps. But just when I was about to stop, something avalanched inside—my tired legs started to run. I charged up the slope like a rampaging bear. Lungs swelled; feet flew. I bounded over rocks and tore up through a stand of trees. I tripped over a rock and fell, sliding down. . . . I extended a leg and a rock stopped me. I pushed up and ran on. *Next rock*—past it. *Next one*—gone! *To that tree*—but my legs buckled. I fell onto my side and crooked an arm around the tree trunk.

Chest heaved. Heart hammered. Snowflakes sputtered on my face. There was an open view. I looked out over the sea at the many islands. I didn't want to move. I wanted it to be that way forever: jade jewels set in turquoise with breaking lace. Sun and snow at the same time with breath and heart the only sounds.

A cliché from a high school teacher floated up in my mind: "Everyone finds their little niche in life," he said with such resignation. I balked at those words, that milquetoast of a man. *Never a niche. Be the entire mountain!*

I thought of how we live in an age of lesser men. We have cut ourselves off from Nature—from extreme experiences. We now only experience the comfortable middle, and something essential in us has atrophied.

I thought of the mountain men—white men who lived Indian. As I lay there, chest pressed to the earth, I felt kin to Bridger, Colter, Jedediah Smith, Jeremiah Johnson. *Like them—sky for my ceiling, mountains for my walls.*

I thought of John Muir roaming the wilds, living on bread crumbs, sleeping in a bear coat. *Like Muir—this is home. Home is not the house—"putting down roots." If you yourself are rooted, you can plant yourself anywhere and grow.*

When my body had cooled, I stood up and started back down. As I plunged back down the slope everything appeared fresh and new, as if I were seeing it for the first time. My body, my being, did not end at my skin—I continued on into everything.

My name formed on my lips and I laughed. *Call me Bird, Bear, Whale, Snail. Call me Ishmael.*

I thought of the Indians who went alone up the mountain to learn their true name. I pondered the name of a Zen monk: Hakuyu—"White Obscurity." I thought of Saint Francis's brotherhood with all living things. In the city I had passed it off as romantic balderdash. On the hill, I thought of how real it is when the spirit is unshackled.

When I stepped out onto the beach I entered another world. A strange haze had descended, as if the clouds had fallen down to earth. The fog was full of glare that pained the eyes.

I couldn't make out the sea. I turned around—the forest wasn't there! I looked down. The beach was disappearing, rocks dissolving. . . . I raised a hand to my eyes to establish reality. The skin was translucent. Less a hand, more like solid-shaped light.

I swung around in a circle, searching. The sky was the sea was the earth was the sky.

Silence roared in my ears like the sea in a shell. My snug feeling of solitude was replaced by stark loneliness. I felt fear grip my spine.

Then I remembered up in the Rocky Mountains skiing into a whiteout: that had to be the explanation. Fear loosened its hold, making room for awe at this Inside Passage that produced weather with a will of its own, that after seducing you with beauty would shake you with fear. An unpredictable place that kept you always prepared, honed to the keen edge of life.

I picked up a long stick and walked like a blind man, probe swinging out front, ears alert for the announcement of water. After the splash, I squatted down and placed the stick on the edge of the liquid light. It disappeared. The tide was going out.

I followed my footprints back to the battered tree, tugged the skiff out, and dragged it down to the sea. I shoved the boat out and jumped in. With the shore obliterated, I could not see the land fall away. Only by dipping my fingers in the water did I know I was moving.

From the perspective of common sense, launching now was the most foolish thing I have ever done. I should have waited for the haze to lift. I could have been swept, sight unseen, past Swanson Island out to open sea. However, I wasn't thinking from a viewpoint that common or that made sense.

I simply felt a loan of Power and trusted in it.

Sweeping tide shook the skiff. I closed my eyes, useless anyway, to concentrate all of myself in my ears, listening . . . silence . . . hollow silence. Then from afar a faint murmur . . . a gurgling . . . *the funnel between No Name and Swanson!*

The tidal river slapped the edge of No Name Island in my right ear; in my left, I heard it cut against Swanson. To avoid the rocks, I oared to midway between the sounds. As the boat surged into the gap I heard my voice sing a song, from the Sioux, that I didn't know I knew:

> "Clear the Way
> In a Sacred Manner I come,
> The earth is mine."

The boat shot out into Freshwater Bay. I felt the openness on my face. I oared out of the tide, spotted the beach with my ears, and aimed for the center.

One December night, I lay in bed waiting for sleep, but the darkness was too alive. Wide awake, I listened to the wolves howling over Breakfast Bay. I threw off the quilt, dressed, and went outside. Up high there was a wind, a motion not present at ground level. The sea, the trees, were still—but clouds rolled and the stars seemed to tremble.

I walked out onto the beach and built a fire with driftwood scraps. I sat back and followed blue and orange mineral-sparks as they lifted into the night.

Cold drafts slid down the mountains, drenching the air with glaciers, pine trees, granite.

As the wolf ululations fell away, I realized that I had undergone metamorphosis. In the underside of the fire I saw the shadow of my past self and knew I had been more alone in the city surrounded by people than being a hermit on a far-flung island.

I thought of Melville's term, *Isolato*—people content to be cut off, cast away, free to explore the universe within. I thought of how it was when Malloff and Beth returned from a lengthy business trip. I never knew when they would reappear. Suddenly the speedboat would cut into the bay: "*Whhwooooo-eeee.*" Malloff would spout his killer whale call. I would row out to meet them. In that vast space and long absence, their faces stood out with all the force of Mount Rushmore. We would share a long, happy evening, with Beth placing beer, lamb chops, chocolate, cigars in front of me. As they announced the latest news—Hollywood movies, football standings, changing of politicians—all the changes would seem to matter little on the timeless island.

I thought of how while Malloff and Beth were on the island I never took them for granted—for I knew they would soon be off traveling again. The island had become a place for them to recharge before stepping back into the wheeling, dealing big business arena. Malloff was trying to market a new "Will Mill" in a big way. When the speedboat pulled away, sadness would touch me; but then I would pick up the maul and make that noun an active verb, attacking the firewood rounds like a mad samurai. As long as I was in motion, the sadness couldn't grab hold. In the evening, after supper, I would sit deep in the chair, puffing the last White Owl cigar, once again content in being an Isolato.

I poked the crumbling beach fire with a stick, and a shower of sparks ascended. They died up in the wind, but I watched a lone mote glow brighter as it climbed higher.

The cold pressed in, stilling my mind. The fire was down to a few embers that flickered like melting candles. I watched the solid rim of tide creep closer. A rivulet poured down a gash in the sand, snuffing the light.

I went inside and sat at the table. In the darkness I watched the frost etch slivered lines on the windows. I felt ready for my second winter. I had learned that out in nature there is no such thing as security, but yet I felt content, knowing that with hard work and forceful dreams one can stay ahead of winter's clench.

In the early morning, I flattened the hoarfrost as I

crunched across the raft to the parked dory, my breath stabbing into the iron air.

Over deep water, I stopped the boat. Baiting my hook, out in the north wind, I heard a line from *Moby Dick:* "Hish! Hish! God goes 'mong the world blackberrying. . . ."

POSTSCRIPT

I departed from the island during my second season of monsoons, in quest of two distant attractions: sunshine and interactions with the female sex. However, for the re-entry from solitude to civilization I should have gone to a "halfway house"—a small, rural settlement like Mendocino or Montauk. Instead, I flew to Miami, Florida, to rekindle an old flame.

When I got off the plane I was in shock. All of my senses that had grown wide open in the natural world were then barraged and blitzed by noise, pollution, tangled expressways, billboards, towering hotels—even concrete felt weird to walk on. . . . All of these were hard-and-fast norms I had lived by before, so much so that I had grown numb to them—but then my eighteen months in the Inside Passage were so awakening and expansive as to nearly erase my previous memory.

I felt like a stranger in a strange land. I could have

been a Martian who crash-landed on Miami Beach—the two worlds were that far apart. Cynthia felt as if she were sheltering a wild mutant, a Sasquatch of sorts. My wardrobe consisted of woolly, smoke-scented sweaters and threadbare long underwear—hardly the attire for Florida; my hair was creeping down past my shoulders; and to sleep at night I had to bunk out on the balcony, for the high-rise apartment felt like a padded cell. For my first three days, while Cynthia was at work, I sat watching reruns of "Charlie's Angels" and "The Price Is Right," acclimatizing to American culture. Cynthia brought me strange concoctions for dinner—like lox and bagels, and fast food—that I ate slowly, as if tasting it all for the very first time.

We then left Miami, making our way across the United States, giving slide lectures on Inside Passage wildlife, scenery, and Kwakiutl Indians to schools for a small honorarium—just enough to carry us to the next engagement. I walked into gymnasiums packed with a thousand restless, nearly out-of-control kids—but when the lights went off and the eagles, Orcas, and Indians came on, there was an hour of silence, followed by such an outpouring of intelligent questions that the principal often called off classes for the rest of the afternoon so that the island storyteller could "teach" geography, history, and biology.

When we reached California, we rented a cheap flat in San Francisco. Driven by an unavoidable desire to communicate the wilderness experiences to the civilized world, I bought a secondhand typewriter, and for the next year attempted to answer my original question: But what on earth to write about . . . ?

ACKNOWLEDGMENTS

My thanks are due, first and foremost, to Will Malloff, who introduced me to entirely new worlds that I will spend all of my life exploring. I'm grateful to Lou and Eleanor Crabe, Michael and Maureen Berry, and Alec Stuart for their warm hospitality along a cold coast; to the fishing wizard, Billy Proctor, for taking me aboard his *Twilight Rock;* to George Dyson, for the use of one of his incomparable baidarkas; and to Beth Erickson, for her wild spirit that infused all of her photographs.

My special thanks to Daniel Bial, editor extraordinaire, and to Elizabeth Pomada and Michael Larsen, the finest literary agents and advisors a writer could have. I want to especially thank Cynthia Cooper, who believed in and supported the author and the book—when both were in the formative stages. I'm grateful to the Latimers: Rebecca, Fred, and Douglas, who read and commented on early drafts of the manuscript, and to Douglas, who taught me how to run ultra-marathons in the mountains of California—great therapy to balance long stints at the typewriter. Thanks to Dessa Brashear and Carol Tarlow, who felt certain that this (publication) would happen; to Nori and Jacquetta Nisbet, for opening up themselves and their Point Reyes home—both provided rejuvenation and inspiration; to Galen Rowell, for his friendship and showing me, through his own books, the joys of adventure and the growth in exceeding one's limits; to "Ishi," the injured bald eagle at the San Francisco Zoo, who allowed me to sit with him one day—taking me back to the Inside Passage when I needed it most; and to Joselle McDowell, with whom I traveled a universe by staying in one place.